Running Your Own Cooperative

running your own
COOPERATIVE

A guide to the setting up of worker
and community owned enterprises

John Pearce

**THE
KOGAN PAGE
Working for Yourself
SERIES**

First published in Great Britain in 1984
by Kogan Page Ltd
120 Pentonville Road
London N1 9JN

British Library Cataloguing in Publication Data

Pearce, John
    Running your own cooperative
    1. Cooperative societies
    I. Title
    334'.6   HD5650

    ISBN 0-85038-789-2
    ISBN 0-85038-790-6 Pbk

Phototypeset by Kerrypress Ltd, Luton

Printed in Great Britain by Anchor Press Ltd
and bound by William Brendon & Son Ltd
both of Tiptree, Essex

Contents

Foreword

Since the middle of the 1970s there has been in Britain a sustained and growing interest in co-operation as a means of organising work and as a way of creating jobs. In part this growth has been a search for alternative ways of working that reflect the desire to get away from confrontational problems in industry and a preference for smaller and more human work organisations. In part the growth has been an attempt to counter rising unemployment by creating new jobs and salvaging some old ones. The survival rate of co-operatives has been good. The evidence suggests that fewer cooperatives fail during the crucial first two years than do conventionally owned and organised small businesses. A number of diverse strands of thinking have led - sometimes separately, sometimes together - to the recent growth in the cooperative way of economic development:

- Many have become disenchanted with the management v. work-force conflict which is seen to be a feature of conventionally organised industry and business.
- There has been a strong reaction against the 'economy of scale' which has created large and insensitive corporations and led growing numbers of people to an espousal of the 'small is beautiful' notion.
- The 'alternative' movement of the 1960s and 1970s focused significantly on new forms of collective ownership and organisation.
- Movement towards a more egalitarian society in which all should have an equal chance has

raised questions about a system of economic organisation which continues to deny the majority an 'as of right' share of the profit of their labour.

☐ Ideas of participation in local social and community matters have been paralleled by a growing wish for a greater democratic 'say' in the affairs of industry and commerce.

☐ Persistent high unemployment, especially in areas where the local economic base seems virtually to have been destroyed, has encouraged experiment with alternative forms of job creation of which cooperatives have been one.

☐ Workers made redundant and with no prospect of re-employment turn to the idea of cooperation and common ownership, often as a last desperate attempt to save their jobs.

This book aims to give basic introductory information to people who are thinking about setting up a cooperative which will create employment. It deals with two particular forms of cooperative: the worker cooperative (sometimes called common ownership enterprise) and the community cooperative (sometimes called community business), both of which are business organisations run on cooperative principles.

No book can really hold all the answers about how to do it: it can only provide guidance, act as a checklist and report on the experience of others which might be useful. This work is written for all those who decide to try. There is too much evidence of caution in our society and an over-strong fear of failure. In business, failures are the inevitable corollary of success. Only those who try can fail – or succeed.

Many people have helped considerably in the preparation of this book and I am grateful to them. In particular I must thank my colleague, Duncan McTavish, who has read and commented valuably on the draft text. Alex Dunlop and Ian Swinney have given detailed guidance on Chapters 5 and 7 respectively. Linda Echlin has helped make sure that what is written is understandable. To them all I owe my thanks.

Especial thanks are due also to Sheila Millar. She has not only turned pages of ill-formed hand writing into neat and correct typescript with remarkable speed, she has also acted as research assistant and general organiser. Without her excellent help the production of this book would have been a much more lengthy and laborious task.

Finally I must thank all my colleages in the Local Enterprise Advisory Project for their forbearance during those weeks in the summer when I was not much in the office.

John Pearce
Local Enterprise Advisory Project
Paisley College
October 1983

Chapter 1
What are Cooperatives?

Cooperatives are associations of people freely joining together to achieve their mutually agreed aims. Worker cooperatives and community cooperatives are about joining together to make a business: to trade, to create jobs and wealth, and usually also to meet certain social objectives in terms of how the business is run and of benefiting the local community.

A workers' cooperative is usually defined as a 'business owned and controlled by the people working in it' which means that all those who work for the enterprise are entitled to be members (sometimes after a probationary period). Ultimate control of the enterprise is on a one person–one vote basis and the principal beneficiaries of the business are the workers, first through having a job, and second through being entitled to a share in any profits.

A community cooperative is defined by the Highlands and Islands Development Board in Scotland as 'a multi-functional business run for the benefit of a local community. It is directly owned and controlled by the people of the community in which it operates, in accordance with cooperative principles'. It is based on a geographical community rather than a working community and membership is usually open to all who live in that area with ultimate control being on the one member–one vote basis. The beneficiaries are the local residents who obtain employment and the community itself through the local application of (future) profits and in some cases through the provision of certain local services.

Definitions which deal with people and human organisation can never be exact as there are always exceptions to any attempt to pigeon-hole. There are examples of cooperatives which are effectively a hybrid between worker and community cooperatives in that they combine workers and representatives of the local community as members. In Chapter 7 we shall return to definitions and key characteristics and examine further the distinctions between enterprises owned and controlled by the work-force and enterprises based on community ownership and control.

Industrial Common Ownership

In 1971 the Industrial Common Ownership Movement (ICOM) was formed out of an organisation called Demintry (Society for Democratic Integration in Industry). ICOM's object was to 'achieve democratic control of their work by people at work' and its 1975 pamphlet listed 13 member firms and another dozen 'moving towards a common ownership structure'. In the same year the Cooperative Union, a servicing body for the whole of the traditional cooperative movement, listed 22 worker producer cooperatives as registered with them. By February 1983 ICOM reported 'one new worker cooperative being formed every working day' with a probable UK total of more than 700 registered worker cooperatives.

In 1976 ICOM's approved set of model rules for registering a worker cooperative society made the legal formation of a cooperative cheap and straightforward and removed from newly formed groups complex and expensive legal problems with limited liability and structure. In 1975 David Watkins MP sponsored a private member's bill in the House of Commons which was enacted in November 1976: the Industrial Common Ownership Act. This established a legal definition of a worker cooperative or common ownership and made a small loan fund (£250,000) available especially for start-up cooperatives. This fund was administered by Industrial Common Ownership Finance Ltd (ICOF), established in 1973 by ICOM as an independent finance company to handle and make loans to worker cooperatives. In 1978 the (Labour) government established a national Cooperative Development Agency with a remit to give advice, information and education, and to carry out research into the 'new wave' of worker and community cooperatives in particular.

Definition of a cooperative: ICO Act 1976

Common ownership enterprises and cooperative enterprises.

2.—(1) For the purposes of this Act a common ownership enterprise is a body as to which the registrar has given, and has not revoked, a certificate stating that he is satisfied—

    (a) that the body is—
- (i) a company which has no share capital, is limited by guarantee and is a bona fide cooperative society; or
- (ii) a society registered or deemed to be registered under the Industrial and Provident Societies Acts 1965 to 1975; and

    (b) that the memorandum or articles of association or rules of the body include provisions which secure—
- (i) that only persons who are employed by, or by a subsidiary of, the body may be members of it, that (subject to any provision about qualifications for membership which is from time to time made by the members of the body by reference to age, length of service or other factors of any description which do not discriminate between persons by reference to politics or religion) all such persons may be members of the body and that members have equal voting rights at meetings of the body,
- (ii) that the assets of the body are applied only for the purposes of objects of the body which do not

include the making over of assets to any member of the body except for value and except in pursuance of arrangements for sharing the profits of the body among its members, and

(iii) that, if on the winding up or dissolution of the body any of its assets remain to be disposed of after its liabilities are satisfied, the assets are not distributed among its members but are transferred to such a common ownership enterprise or such a central fund maintained for the benefit of common ownership enterprises as may be determined by the members at or before the time of the winding up or dissolution or, in so far as the assets are not so transferred, are held for charitable purposes; and

(c) that the body is controlled by a majority of the people working for the body and of the people working for the subsidiaries, if any, of the body.

(2) For the purposes of this Act a co-operative enterprise is a body as to which the Secretary of State has given, and has not revoked, a certificate stating that he is satisfied that—

(a) having regard to the provision which is made by the written constitution of the body as to the manner in which the income of the body is to be applied for the benefit of its members and all other relevant provisions of the constitution, the body is in substance a cooperative association; and

(b) the body is controlled by a majority of the people working for the body and of the people working for the subsidiaries, if any, of the body.

Local cooperative development

Developments at national level have stimulated local growth and vice versa. A network of cooperative development agencies has emerged to give advice, support and professional guidance. First established in 1977 was the Scottish Cooperatives Development Committee, initially with financial support from the Department of Industry and the Cooperative Union, and now funded mainly by the Scottish Development Agency and local authorities. The other 60 local cdas cover various geographical areas and are mostly funded by local authority grants. Some local authorities have appointed their own cooperative development officers while others have made available funds for lending to cooperatives in their particular area. In 1983 the Welsh TUC launched a Cooperative Resource Centre based in Cardiff with Welsh Development Agency and EEC funding. The majority of local agencies have been initially set up to concentrate on assisting with the formation of worker cooperatives but some are now including both worker and community cooperatives in their remit.

In Britain worker cooperatives are essentially small businesses run cooperatively by the people who work in them. Many include in their aims a commitment to help the wider community beyond their own business, but business survival is the primary objective. Many worker cooperatives have come about in response to unemployment or redundancy and in some areas the encouragement of cooperatives is an integral part of a policy to stimulate new business formation and thus jobs. In other areas, local authorities take a more political stance, favouring cooperatives as the type of business structure of which they would like to see more. As part of a job creation strategy the formation of worker cooperatives depends on businesses being established which can survive commercially.

Mondragon

A source of considerable inspiration for cooperative growth and development has been the example of the Mondragon group of cooperatives in the Basque region of Spain. There, since 1956 when five engineers under the guidance of their local priest founded the first cooperative manufacturing paraffin cookers, a federation has been built up which employs more than 17,000 workers in over 80 different businesses. All the cooperative businesses are linked to a cooperative bank which they own and receive business and financial guidance from a central financial services body which they also own. This body not only guides existing cooperative businesses in the group but is responsible for planning and examining ideas for new cooperatives. As well as productive enterprises the group also runs commercial services including the local food supermarket, runs a higher educational and technical college, provides housing, and organises a social security system. The Mondragon group of cooperatives allocate some profit to community benefit purposes and through their involvement in social and educational services, as well as job and wealth creation, they are as much community cooperatives as they are worker-owned enterprises.

Community cooperatives

These have been developed in Britain as a particular strategy relevant to areas of especially high unemployment and to parts of the country which have become economically marginal.

During 1975 and 1976 many communities in the Western Isles became involved in local projects under the Job Creation Programme to create short-term jobs. The Highlands and Islands Development Board decided to try and build on this evidence of local initiative, and towards the end of 1977 announced their community cooperative programme. The HIDB scheme included the appointment of field workers to explain the programme and assist local steering groups plan their enterprises; it provided for establishment grants matching one pound for every pound raised locally, management grants to help subsidise the cooperatives in their early years and access to normal HIDB grant and loan assistance. This programme – arguably the most radical strategy for local economic development yet seen in Britain – has resulted in the formation of a dozen cooperatives throughout the Highlands and Islands with others at present in the formation stages.

The HIDB programme acted as an inspiration to many groups in other parts of Britain. In old industrial areas, blighted inner cities and peripheral housing estates are communities with local economies now almost as marginal as those in remote rural areas, with exceptionally high rates of unemployment (50 per cent adult unemployment is not untypical: it is often higher for young people) and with the added problems of scale and increasing lack of skill. In such areas community groups and organisations had also gained experience of trading and employing people through the Job Creation Programme and were looking for ways of taking action in their areas to create jobs which might last, wealth which might be recycled and at the same time provide services which were needed locally. The result has been the community business – the urban equivalent of the community cooperative.

Local economic development
In Scotland a federal network of community businesses, Community Business Scotland, has been established to lobby for resources and provide a nationwide information exchange. The CBS definition of a community business is generally recognised as the basic working description.

A community business is a *trading organisation* which is set up, *owned and controlled by the local community* and which aims to create *ultimately self-supporting jobs for local people*, and to be a focus for *local development*. Any profits made from its business activities go either to create *more employment*, or to provide local services or to assist other schemes of *community benefit*.

Community businesses are particularly in evidence in Central Scotland where in Strathclyde Region the Local Enterprise Advisory Project has been funded since 1978 to advise and assist local groups plan and set them up.

In Wales, Antur Broyd Cymru (Welsh Community Enterprise) promotes both worker and community cooperatives. The national CDA has developed model rules for a neighbourhood services cooperative (a hybrid version of a workers' cooperative which allows some community participation) and more recently for community-based cooperatives. Local authorities throughout Britain have followed the example set by the HIDB and Strathclyde Region and refer to community-owned enterprise as well as worker-owned enterprise in their strategic planning statements and are funding community business development units. Local cooperative development agencies are advising on the formation of community enterprises when these appear more appropriate than a workers' cooperative.

Community ownership

The community enterprise (cooperative or business) has evolved as a strategy to generate economic activity in areas of high unemployment and where the local economy is weak or virtually non-existent. Membership is open to the residents of a particular locality (sometimes it will be linked to the membership of a pre-existing community association). The enterprise will almost certainly be multi-functional in that it will be responsible for a number of specific projects at any one time. It will both initiate business ideas and help local people develop their own ideas; it may intervene in various ways in the local economy; it may sponsor

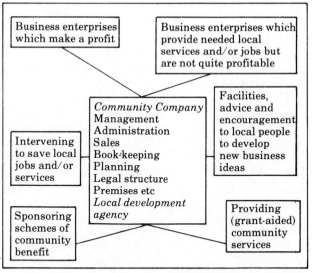

1. Holding company and development agency

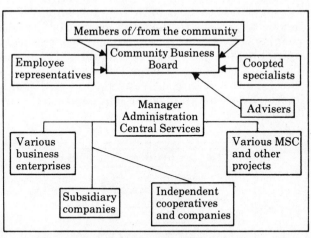

2. Operational and ownership structure of a community business

projects of community benefit in addition to its own trading activities and business development work. It is likely to be both holding company and local development agency (Figure 1) and seek to

19

provide a community-owned structure in a particular locality which can initiate economic activity on behalf of the residents. Some community-grown specific enterprises might in time be floated off as self-standing businesses, likely as worker cooperatives.

The community business is thus more than a trading organisation, it is a means of stimulating new business growth in areas and among people where there is little or no tradition of entrepreneurial activity and usually a history of long-term unemployment and social deprivation.

Worker ownership

The workers' cooperative is typically a monofunctional enterprise run by a group of workers primarily for their own benefit through having a job with reasonable pay and good conditions. Owned and controlled by its members on a one person–one vote basis, only persons employed in the enterprise are usually permitted to be members. Membership is open to all workers as of right. There can be no external holding of equity in a workers' cooperative: a fundamental principle is that labour will hire the capital (that is through loan stock) rather than be hired by capital as in the traditional capitalist business structure of shareholding.

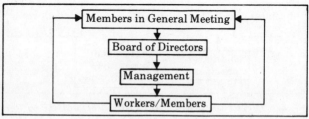

3. Workers' cooperative structure

In order to be viable the workers' cooperative ideally requires all necessary skills within its membership. Local cooperative development agencies can provide guidance and assistance but that is no long-term alternative to in-house capability. Eventually, federations might develop to provide jointly controlled specialist services and functions. As yet, despite the significant growth of numbers in recent years, there are no major examples of groups of cooperatives federating in this way. The community enterprise attempts to provide central services to a number of businesses and projects, but at a very micro level. Most workers' cooperatives will have social objectives and commitments in their constitution to benefit the local community in some way.

Chapter 2
First Steps

There are three starting points for a workers' cooperative:

☐Starting from scratch.
☐Coming from a redundancy situation.
☐Converting from an existing privately owned business.

New starts

These come about in a number of ways. Ideally, a group of people with a good business idea, all the necessary skills and a commitment to working cooperatively form the basis of each new co-operative. In practice one or more dimension is often missing to begin with. A group might want to form a cooperative but not have a business idea, or they may have an idea but not all the necessary skills. In other situations an individual has an idea and wants to form a cooperative group around him or herself. Whatever the point of initiation, the first steps must be to bring together *idea, people and the wish to cooperate*.

Starting with people

Most usually it is the people who come first: they want to set up a business and form a cooperative, and they have given the matter some thought before coming through the door of their local cooperative development agency. For such groups the next steps are:

1. To look in detail at what being in a cooperative means to make sure that they do, in fact, want to form one; and

2. To do a feasibility study to see if their idea can be viable.

For a new group coming together for the first time to consider forming a cooperative, it is important to set about gathering information systematically. Regular meetings of the founding members begin to make the cooperative idea real and, even in the very early planning stages, it is useful to establish some basic structure by having someone to co-ordinate discussion and someone to act as secretary to record what is agreed. It is particularly important to be clear who is going to take what follow-up action after each meeting.

The officers of the local cda should be a first call for information and advice. Where there is no local cda there are national organisations such as the Cooperative Development Agency (CDA) and the Industrial Common Ownership Movement (ICOM) (see Appendix 1). While thinking about your own cooperative it can be useful to talk to others who have already set one up, find out from them the problems they encountered and how they tackled them. There are now also a number of case studies about cooperatives which can give further insight into what lies ahead (see Appendix 2).

Starting with ideas
There has been some experience of local development agencies initiating cooperatives by identifying a potentially viable product or service, carrying out a feasibility study and then recruiting people from the labour market to come and join the new business. The initial emphasis is on business viability with the workers in the new enterprise having to learn about cooperation and what that involves after they start work. Both the Scottish Cooperatives Development Committee and Bootstrap Enterprises in London have attempted this model and report some success but also a lengthy involvement of development staff to provide support and guidance. Bootstrap is a form of community business aiming to create jobs for the

23

long-term unemployed in newly created small worker cooperatives, and arranges a detailed training programme for the new employees of each cooperative. That programme includes learning about their potential business and being a cooperative.

Bootstrap Enterprises

Bootstrap Enterprises is a Hackney-based project concerned with tackling the problems of high unemployment. Bootstrap is a company limited by guarantee and a registered charity. Its aims are first, to improve the job prospects of the unskilled unemployed by providing them with technical and business management training, and second, to create new and permanent jobs in the borough by promoting worker-controlled business.

Bootstrap consists of a number of small workshops where new cooperative businesses can start up in sheltered circumstances, full-time staff to examine business ideas and give advice, guidance and support and to provide training and a very small cooperative development loan fund. Bootstrap embryo businesses number five so far: cycle repairs, typing, knitting, TV repairs and a snack bar. One early business, a jewellery workshop, has been closed down. There is a shared retail shop on the premises and two small workshops are let on a commercial basis to two independent new small businesses.

In some cases, Bootstrap businesses have started with a pre-existing group or individual with an idea but more recently Bootstrap has been identifying a viable business idea first and then recruiting a group of local unemployed people to set up the business under Bootstrap guidance and with a prepared training programme. All Bootstrap businesses start on the basis of no wages until the business can afford to pay them. Creche facilities are available daily from 10am to 3pm.

Each embryo business has to agree to certain conditions of support which are laid down by Bootstrap in a formal letter. These conditions specify such details as the cooperative structure to be adopted by the new business, the frequency of meetings with Bootstrap staff and of the cooperative members themselves, the tenancy of workshop space, the preparation of an agreed business and financial plan, any loan agreement, the provision of monthly management and

monitoring of accounts, the wages policy for the
cooperative and how profits might be distributed.
  Bootstrap Enterprises is partly financed by Hackney
Council through the Inner City Partnership Fund and
partly by various national and local charities and
businesses. Two full-time and three part-time workers
are employed to run the project.

Promoting the idea

All cooperative development agencies engage in
promotional work, informing people in their area
about cooperation and sowing ideas. This is done
by speaking at meetings, arranging conferences
and seminars, exhibitions, producing leaflets and
posters, making video films and slide/tape
presentations and using the local press, radio and
television. Some cdas have advertised in the local
press for people wanting to set up a cooperative
and others built up registers of interested people,
recording skills and other relevant details in an
attempt to help appropriate groups come together
and match people with complementary skills.

Redundancy cooperatives

Redundancies have been a common feature of
economic life in recent years and where jobs are
declared lost, the workers' natural reaction is to
look for some way of saving them. In this context
the idea of forming a cooperative often comes late,
after other avenues have been explored (resisting
the threatened closure, for example) and can be
more a last-ditch attempt to salvage something
rather than a positive wish to create a cooperative.
Experience of turning existing failed capitalist
businesses into cooperatives almost overnight has
not been successful. The circumstances have to be
very special for worker owners to be able to make a
go of a business which private capitalist ownership has decided is not profitable. Markets are
likely to have been run down, machinery to be old,
buildings in need of repair, research and develop-

ment never carried out. The lure of redundancy payments dissipates worker determination to act.

Where there has been some success, however, is in establishing *part* of a failed enterprise as a workers' cooperative. Phoenix Cooperatives,[1] as they have come to be called, take a potentially profitable part of an otherwise failed large enterprise and with an enthusiastic nucleus from the old work-force create a new small business from the ashes of the old. Thus, when Lyons closed their bakery in Glasgow making more than 340 people redundant, a small group of engineers, salesmen and bakers formed a cooperative based on the 'pie flat' making Scotch pies, scones and pancakes which has built its employment up to 40.

When a redundancy situation arises action has to be taken quickly to ascertain if there is the basis for a new business. Because of the speed necessary it is almost essential that the workers involved obtain the help of some external body like a cooperative development agency, local authority industrial development worker or a trades union official. Also because of speed, the emphasis must be on whether there is a potentially viable business, with the cooperative aspects being considered later. The work-force are already in position and in most cases either they or their trades union representatives will have taken the first steps to explore the idea of creating the cooperative.

The first key questions to be answered are:
1. *Is there a market for the goods or services being produced?* In the case of a parent company closing a branch factory, the parent may supply the market from elsewhere, or the market may have collapsed, in which case the question becomes: is there an alternative market or can the factory make something else?

---

1. *Phoenix Cooperatives* is the title of a video film produced by the Scottish Cooperatives Development Committee and also of a booklet published by the national Cooperative Development Agency.

2. *Are all the necessary skills available to run the proposed business?* Often a branch factory has had no sales staff, being a production unit only; or the management may have accepted redundancy or been relocated, leaving just shop-floor workers.
3. *Is enough of the existing work-force committed?* Redundancy payments or other considerations may make key workers decide not to go along with the cooperative idea.

Two other major considerations in developing a Phoenix Cooperative are what happens to the buildings, plant and equipment of the former company and whether the funds required for the enterprise can be raised quickly enough. The constructive cooperation of the original company which is closing down can be a determining factor in helping a new enterprise get started: and by definition their lack of cooperation can effectively block anything happening. In Inchinnan, in the west of Scotland, Dunlop not only made available premises and plant to the Phoenix Cooperative on generous terms but also gave the contract for clearing the remainder of the site to the cooperative, thus providing some guaranteed work for the first crucial six months. Raising finance is dealt with in Chapter 4 but the speed and imagination required in redundancy situations can cause problems with both commercial and public sources of funds.

It is important not to lose sight of the cooperative aspects in a Phoenix Cooperative, although this can be difficult in the haste to salvage the plant and get trading as quickly as possible. Yet a failure to teach the business's members something about cooperative principles, ideals and practices can be to store up management and organisational problems for later.

Randolph Leisurewear

Towards the end of 1980 the Buckhaven, Fife factory of
the Clares Carlton clothing group learned that it was
to close at Christmas with the loss of all 60 jobs.
Realising that other jobs in the area would be
impossible to find and that no one else was going to
rescue them, the manager and some of the largely
female work-force decided, at the suggestion of their
trade union, to try and do it themselves as a workers'
cooperative and approached the Scottish Cooperatives
Development Committee for help.

The factory was a satellite production unit with no
sales capacity or financial control responsibilities. The
Buckhaven production, and thus sales, was to be
transferred to factories in England, but it was clear
that there was a highly skilled and committed work-
force and a production manager who wanted to keep
the business alive. SCDC assisted with negotiations
with Clares Carlton to obtain factory and equipment
rent free for six months and with the SDA for a market
study to be carried out. The cooperative was formed
with ICOM model rules, with 23 of the former work-
force each contributing £100 and agreeing to work for
no wages to start with in order to build up working
capital.

The first months were a hard hand-to-mouth time as
orders were slowly won and fulfilled with the SCDC
workers often acting in the role of salesmen. The work-
force were denied unemployment benefit because they
had chosen to 'pay' themselves nothing and worked
without wages for three months. With financial help
from the SDA the SCDC hired a local person for six
months to work with the cooperative to build up sales
and develop new markets. After this initial period with
the cooperative, he joined as a full member to be the
sales manager.

Eight months after the closure had been announced,
the cooperative had built up a reasonable and growing
order book for its high quality rainwear and industrial
clothing. In the summer of 1981, a contract was
negotiated with a Swedish company to be the sole UK
manufacturer of a range of waterproof garments.

Finance for Randolph Leisurewear, as the
Buckhaven Cooperative is known, has been built up
from the workers' own investment, and loans from
ICOF, the Fife Regional and Kirkcaldy District
Councils, the Scottish Development Agency, and from
the Cooperative Bank under the government's
guarantee scheme. Throughout its development the
cooperative has received regular support and
assistance from the SCDC.

Conversion cooperatives

The best known example of a private business converted into a cooperative is the Scott Bader Commonwealth in Northamptonshire. Scott Bader is a successful chemicals company employing more than 400 people in Britain and Germany, established in 1951 by the late Ernest Bader. Because of his belief in common ownership and sharing the rewards of labour, he gifted his company to be held 'in common' for the workers.

Conversion depends first on the owner's decision to change his private business into a worker ownership and second, successful conversion depends on the work-force wanting to assume the responsibilities of ownership and control. There have been examples of conversion plans being thwarted by the reluctance of the workers involved. Given that the business is already established and viable, in a conversion the key problems relate to developing an understanding of cooperation, the enthusiasm for carrying out the conversion and questions of structure which symbolise the change in ownership and accountability. It is important that the idea of conversion is introduced to all concerned in a way that allows all questions to be tackled step by step and anxieties faced up to. Whereas for the owner conversion may seem an exciting step which is the culmination of years of private thought and discussion, for the average worker in the concern it could appear to be nothing more than unsettling change which barely touches on day-to-day working practice.

Community cooperatives

Community cooperatives and community businesses are established mostly in areas of high unemployment where the starting point is likely to be the question posed by local people: *what can we do to tackle unemployment*? The search for forms of self-help by community groups and the

29

unemployed themselves has gained considerable momentum in the last decade. As practical experience has been gained, more groups have been inspired to try and do something in their own areas: action born of a growing belief that neither public nor private industry will be quick to provide the jobs that are needed and of a preference to do something rather than wait on others' action.

Promoting the idea

In some communities discussion about what can be done starts from an existing community organisation, from a local leader or activist or from an individual, such as a church minister or a community development officer. In other communities, first discussion depends on a stimulus from outside. The HIDB appointed field officers to go and talk with the people in the communities of the Western Isles about the idea of forming community cooperatives. Part of the remit of organisations like the Local Enterprise Advisory Project in Strathclyde and Antur Teifi in Dyfed is to promote the idea of local economic self-help using video films, exhibitions and slide/tape presentations, but most importantly by simply talking with groups of people – community councils, tenants' associations, study groups, action committees – in their neighbourhoods.

Promotion of the idea that action might be possible and constructive can be especially important in areas where past patterns of employment have been to work for others (usually the handful of large local factories) with no history or tradition of entrepreneurship. In such communities of high, often long-term unskilled unemployment, the notion of self-help which will create locally determined jobs requires a considerable change of attitude and the gradual growth of confidence. First steps are thus likely to be slower than in the case of workers' cooperatives as people learn about the very notion of business as something to 'do' oneself rather than be 'done by' others.

The local steering group

However the idea of wanting to do something emerges, the first practical step to be taken is the formation of a local steering group who will start investigating the idea of creating jobs locally and exploring possible ideas. The steering group might be a subcommittee of a tenants' association, an ad hoc group formed by a local activist or community worker, it may be a group of unemployed workers, or come about through a public meeting called to discuss the problem of local unemployment. There are almost as many methods of creating a steering group as there are community cooperatives. The pattern of local organisations and personalities determines how it happens: but the formation of a steering group of some sort which can begin to focus discussion *and* action is essential.

Once set up the steering group has a number of tasks:

1. *Find out what other groups in similar situations have done and how they set about doing it.* There is now some written material about community cooperatives and visual aids available (see Appendices 1 and 2. Arrange to visit existing community cooperatives. When visits are impracticable because of distance or cost, find out what other groups in your area are doing or have been discussing. There are few areas in the country now with no examples of some community-based economic action.

2. *Find ways of involving more people locally.* Make sure that people know what you are thinking and talking about and have a chance to join in and contribute their ideas. Distributing publicity leaflets can be a useful means of publicising the group's work, and writing the leaflets can be a good way of clarifying what it is you think you are doing! A public meeting (or series of meetings) with video tapes about community business or with slides and photographs can help build up interest. Perhaps most important and most valuable in the long term is to go

and talk to the committees of various local organisations.

3. *Find out who can do what for you.* What helping agencies are there in your area? Is there a cooperative development agency that specialises in community cooperatives? What is the attitude of the local authority? Is there a Local Enterprise Trust? Are there community development officers who can help the group, or trades union officials? Is it possible to identify people with professional skills who may be sympathetic to your ideas: an accountant, bank manager, lawyer, businessman?

The process of finding out who can help is also a means of telling people what you are hoping to do. Enlisting sympathy and support at an early stage can help pave the way for real practical help later on. Remember to contact local politicians at all levels.

4. *Find a way for the steering group to turn all its talk and information into action.* Usually that means having an efficient secretary with the time to write letters and make phone calls etc between meetings and a chairperson to ensure that meetings make decisions and that it is clear at the end of each meeting who is going to do what. Ideally the follow-up action should be shared among the group, otherwise you will have an overworked secretary!

5. *Find a suitable process for reporting back to the local community.* That might be simply reporting to a parent organisation's annual general meeting, or setting up a special public meeting; or producing a report, or using the media. However it is done, it is important to ensure that local people continue to be informed and thus involved.

The process of finding out about community cooperatives and community business is in part an educational process which probably involves several members of the steering group learning about business and related matters for the first time. It can be a slow process during which time membership of the steering group might fluctuate until it settles down to a committed nucleus of people with a common notion of what they want to do.

Ideas

Another of these first steps will be to start thinking about possible ideas for the community cooperative (see Chapter 3). There are four main ways of identifying them:

1. *What skills do local people have?* It is an easier task to build a business idea around someone with a recognised skill.
2. *Is it possible to copy or adapt something done by another community business?* Ideas which have been successful in a similar community elsewhere can often be followed, with the benefit of others' experience.
3. *What goods or services are needed in the locality?* In most areas of high unemployment – especially housing estates and remote rural areas – it is not difficult to make a long list of commercial and other services which are lacking and which a community cooperative might set out to provide.
4. *Are there any unused local resources which might form the base for a community cooperative:* a disused school or an empty factory for example; unused land or hard-to-let houses? Sometimes the *social* problem of vandalised buildings which become an eyesore can be the starting point for *business* activity and development.

Planning and starting up a community cooperative can be a slow process, and one which requires patience and some tenacity of purpose. It is a slow process, partly because for most community cooperative groups there is a lot to learn as start-up business activities are for most a new departure, and also because it takes a long time not just to plan but to negotiate the resources which are needed. Outside the Scottish Highlands and Islands there is no tailor-made scheme to give funds and support and so local steering groups have to seek out the resources they need from many different sources.

Because the preliminary stages can be very drawn out, some groups have looked for ways of mixing short-term action with other long-term planning and negotiation. Short-term action means that there is something positive to be done as well as all the talk and meetings and paper work; it demonstrates to local people that this is a serious attempt to achieve something and gives the group members some practical experience. The most experienced businessman will say that the best way of learning is to do it!

Govan Workspace and Govan Enterprises

In 1978 a community project, Govan Area Resource Centre, set up an employment study group of local people to examine the problems facing this shipbuilding part of Glasgow and to consider what action local people might take. Arising from the work of this group, two related community companies have been set up. Both Govan Workspace and Govan Enterprises are companies limited by guarantee and are non profit distributing. Membership is open to any people who live or work locally and some of the present directors of the companies were originally members of the employment study group. Govan Enterprises has charitable status.

Govan Workspace is a property company which provides small scale managed workspaces and, with Govan Enterprises, provides practical advice and assistance to individuals and groups wishing to set up new businesses. Govan Workspace has converted a disused primary school to provide 37 units of between 300 and 600 sq ft. A further and much larger scheme is being carried out in association with the Scottish Development Agency who are converting 80,000 sq ft of a former Lyons Bakery into small industrial units. As the first units become available Govan Workspace will be responsible for letting and managing them.

Govan Enterprises seeks to initiate community-owned trading enterprises and to assist local individuals set up their own small businesses. The

company has tried out a number of business ideas:
wood-stripping, contract cleaning, retailing
wholefoods, jobbing gardening, running a community
market. Two new enterprises have been soundly
established: packaging and distributing a snack food
to the licensed trade and a small printing business
which has now become an independent off-shoot. Both
companies have sponsored a number of short-term
MSC projects. Between them the companies directly
employ over ten people while tenants of the first
workspaces have brought more than 100 jobs into the
area.

Finance for the work of the two companies has come
from: the public sector (urban programme, MSC,
District Council, Scottish Development Agency); the
private sector (Shell UK, National Westminster Bank,
British Shipbuilders) and trusts (Calouste Gulbenkian
Foundation, Joseph Rowntree Social Services Trust).

Pallion Residents Enterprises

Pallion Residents Enterprises is a community company
in Sunderland where local people have taken over a disused and badly vandalised factory which used to make
Hepworths clothing. More than one in every three local
people are out of work, with few prospects and opportunities for the young. The company plans to turn the
84,000 sq ft of factory into an industrial, sports and
leisure complex 'created by and for the people of
Pallion'.

In brief, their plan comprises:

*P*roper jobs, proper training, provision for the future,
in workshops, factory units and business premises of
varying sizes. In all, over 50,000 sq ft of the ground
floor space will be devoted to commercial use.

*A*ll manner of indoor sports facilities, including
portable squash courts, five-a-side football, carpet
bowls, table tennis. A karate club has already
started, cycling and running enthusiasts have
already asked if they may use the premises as their
headquarters, and a commercial cycle speedway
outfit is investigating the viability of a track.

*L*eisure facilities for all groups within the
community, including a coffee bar, licensed bar,
luncheon club for the elderly, creche facilities for
mothers with toddlers, play groups and so on.

*L*inks with local colleges, so that wherever possible,
local youngsters can gain practical experience within
the complex to back up the theory they have learned

on their courses, and thus increase their job chances. *I*nformation on tap on computer terminals, and all manner of information, advice and continuing support for all who use the premises, including a separate centre offering specialist advice for the disabled.

*O*ffice back-up facilities on a cooperative basis. The administrative block on the first floor running the length of one side of the building will offer to take over the tedious, time-consuming paper work for new businesses. The idea is to encourage redundant crafts-men, and others who have never been in business before, to start up on their own, secure in the know-ledge that their administrative and other problems will get expert attention, freeing them to get on with the job they know best.

*N*ew opportunities in training, particularly in high technology so that local people will be equipped with the skills of the future.

Some examples of short-term action include:

☐ *Voluntary trading*. That is, working voluntarily and paying all income into the community business. It is a means of local people contributing their 'sweat equity' and building up some working capital for the business, as well as being a means of testing practically some business ideas.

☐ *Market stalls*. Running a market stall can give valuable trading experience with only small overhead expenses. Some community coopera-tive groups have even run their own regular mini-market in a local hall which gives the chance of trading to a number of different local people and organisations.

☐ *Make-work schemes* by sponsoring schemes or projects under the community programme of the Manpower Services Commission. Although such schemes are designed to be short term and non-commercial they can give useful experience of organising work and introduce potential workers to the community cooperative. There have been several examples of an MSC funded non-commercial project being converted by the community cooperative into a commercial enterprise once the period of grant-funding was over. In this way the period of the MSC scheme becomes part training, part practical feasibility study.

Chapter 3
Ideas and Feasibility Studies

Most worker cooperatives start with a definite idea for a product or service: something which an individual or group of friends have been thinking about for some time or, in the case of redundancy situations and conversions, the business idea is already determined. In community cooperatives where the starting point is more usually *what can we do about unemployment?* rather than *let's start such-and-such business*, there is usually a search for potential ideas focused around the skills people have, what others have done, what needs there are locally and what resources might be available.

Finding ideas

Sometimes it is necessary to look farther afield for a viable idea, and cooperative development agencies have identified ideas, researched them and then set about forming cooperatives around them. A business idea which *works* is a particular formula in a particular set of conditions. There is no simple way of finding ideas: they emerge, sometimes through complex research and development, or by systematically looking for market opportunities, but more often by chance or because someone happens to be able to do something or is in the right place at the right time.

The most common method of finding ideas is to brainstorm, to list anything and everything which comes into your head as you sit around with other members of your group. The resulting list will undoubtedly include things which are crazy and zany, but when the list is re-examined there is likely to be the basis of a firm idea or two which can be further explored. It can be useful to give some framework to a brainstorming session by using a checklist of broad questions:

Are there services which are not being provided in the locality?
Are there goods which are imported but which could be manufactured locally?
Are there people available with particular skills?
Is there subcontract work available?
Are there local businesses about to close because of retirement leaving a gap in local provision?
Is there any chance of obtaining a franchise?
Is there the possibility of taking an agency?
Are there any fringe activities linked to the local large businesses?

Some local cooperative development agencies have advertised in the press for people and/or ideas. Some local authorities maintain rudimentary information about what is going on in their area. Local schools or colleges may be persuaded to do a project on new business ideas. Similarly, business idea competitions can act as a spur to get people to put together thoughts which otherwise get no further than wishful thinking in the pub.

Many cooperatives set up a service rather than a manufacturing business. The market for services is more likely to be local and so it is easier to see if it exists and on what scale. Less equipment and machinery are needed: it is the skill to provide the service that is important.

Manufacturing depends on the ability to make something which no one else makes at all, or to make it more cheaply, and/or better than others. Money and time are needed to research and develop product ideas and then to test market them. Compared with a service business it is harder to ascertain the extent of the possible market. The cost of starting production in terms of machinery, materials and premises will demand considerable start-up capital and there will usually be a longer gap before receiving payment for goods made than for services rendered.

Enterprise workshops

Because it is more difficult to develop manufacturing ideas some local authorities have devised methods of providing special assistance during the research and development stage. *New Enterprise Workshops* (variously called New Venture Workshops or Innovation Workshops) provide workshop space, storage, some basic machinery and equipment – for example in machining, metal working, joinery, electrical and electronic work – and supervisors with a range of technical skills. People with new product ideas can make use of the facilities, usually for limited periods up to one year, in order to develop their idea to the prototype stage. This crucial research and development sorts out technical problems and begins the process of establishing the existence of a market. Such New Enterprise Workshops are usually open as long as possible during the week so that they can be used by the employed and the unemployed alike. Experience has shown that the manager of such a workshop is a key figure, not only for his encouragement of users but also for his ability to find sources of technical advice, second-hand machinery and free materials. Some community cooperatives have begun to adapt the new enterprise workshop idea to the neighbourhood. They provide rudimentary workshop space and equipment to encourage people who ordinarily would never think of putting up a business idea to come forward and share their ideas with others and to develop them.

The city of Sheffield has established a product development company with members of the University and Polytechnic, and the Greater London Enterprise Board expects to set up a Product Development Centre in north London particularly to sponsor socially useful products.

Whereas the New Enterprise Workshop provides a service to people with projects to develop, other local authorities have established units especially to seek out business ideas and work them up into viable packages which can be taken on by an existing cooperative or one especially created for the purpose. Searching for new product ideas among shop-floor workers was pioneered by the Lucas Aerospace Shop Stewards Combine Committee[1] and further developed by the Centre for Alternative Industrial and Technological Systems (CAITS).[2] They believed – and it has been borne out – that there must be a rich seam of ideas among people on the factory floor which ordinarily go no further than idle talk at dinner time.

Forgewood Enterprises

Forgewood is a housing estate to the north of Motherwell with a population around 8,000. It is an area where unemployment is estimated to be at least 30 per cent. Many of the population are unskilled and there is a high incidence of housing and social difficulties. It is deemed by Strathclyde Region to be in need of 'priority treatment'.

Forgewood Enterprises is a multi-purpose community company, limited by guarantee and with charitable status. It grew out of the determination of a small group of local people, some of them former local councillors, to try and do something positive to tackle both unemployment and other community problems. The main purposes of Forgewood Enterprises are to stimulate more economic activity in the area and initiate a number of community-owned enterprises. In its first year the company established a local network of home knitters and sewers and has begun to develop markets for them; it has set up a caneware retail

1. In 1979 the Lucas Workers Group produced a comprehensive alternative plan for parts of Lucas Aerospace which suggested a range of socially useful products as a means of saving jobs and shifting company activities out of the arms industry. *Turning industrial decline into expansion – a trade union initiative:* interim report by Lucas Aerospace Confederation Trade Union Committee: February 1979.

2. CAITS grew out of the need of the Lucas Shop Stewards Committee for research and support for their alternative plan proposals. The Centre has developed a creative approach to employment generation through new product development and has worked closely with cooperative development agencies. See Appendix 1: Sources of help and advice.

operation, provided space and assistance for the local
community café, sponsored an MSC gardening project
for adults and started exploring the potential for a
jobbing gardening and landscaping business.

The Enterprise is based in a block of six council
houses owned by Motherwell District. Within this block
the company is establishing a *local enterprise
workshop* which acts as a centre for local unemployed
people to meet, exchange ideas, obtain information and
begin to work up possible business ideas. The
workshop will provide small workspaces and some
tools and equipment which can be used for developing
prototypes or indeed taking first tentative trading
steps. The company's full-time manager will provide
advice and information to individuals or groups
wanting to start up an enterprise. Training courses will
be arranged and assistance given with book-keeping,
VAT, tax etc. The local enterprise workshop is
attempting to generate the idea of enterprise and self-
employment in an area where people have traditionally
worked for a large company – mostly in iron and steel
manufacture – and it does this by providing practical
help and guidance at the neighbourhood level. New
businesses which emerge from this process will either
operate as part of the multi-purpose community
company or be floated off independently.

Is the idea feasible?

Having found an idea the potential workers or
community cooperative group have to work out if it
is feasible. The first stages of any feasibility study
are really no more than straightforward common-
sense and best done by the people who are to be
involved. Later on it may be necessary to bring in
some experts but it is not necessary to make the
process more complicated and mysterious than it
need be. Essentially doing a feasibility study and
preparing a business plan is *how you find out if
your idea will work.*

Clydeclean

One strategy employed by the Scottish Cooperatives
Development Committee in its Clydeside Project
(funded by the urban programme through Strathclyde
Region) has been to identify a potentially viable
business idea and then develop a cooperative around it.

Office and factory contract cleaning in Glasgow was identified as one possible area of work in 1980 and a cooperative set up. The founder members of the Clydeclean Cooperative were SCDC workers and committee members and the SCDC worker responsible for Clydeclean acted both as entrepreneur and manager. He won the first contracts, hired the first workers and organised the work of the cooperative – including working alongside the first cleaners.

During the first year the emphasis was on building up the Clydeclean business as a profitable operation and gradually increasing the participation of the workers in running the business. By the end of 1981 there were seven cleaners working in three different locations with the cleaners handling their own wages through a bank account for each contract or set of contracts. Bi-monthly meetings of all the cleaners were held to discuss the affairs of the cooperative and invoicing and book-keeping had just been taken on by one of the workers. Slowly a cohesive group of workers was beginning to emerge but the SCDC development worker retained a key management role especially with regard to sales and estimating and the affairs of the cooperative were overseen by the SCDC's Clydeside subcommittee.

One year later at the end of 1982 the number of workers had risen to 16 working on eight contracts. A cooperative manageress had been employed and the focus of day-to-day and strategic management decisions had shifted from the SCDC worker to the manageress and the cooperative cleaners. The non-working founder members remained as the legal members of the cooperative while discussions continued about the exact structure of the cooperative in the future: whether Clydeclean should be a workers' cooperative with its workers organised in autonomous work groups based around particular contracts throughout the city, or become a second-tier marketing and servicing cooperative with the contract-based work groups being established as separate workers' cooperatives in their own right.

What resources do you have?

Stage 1. Look carefully at the resources which your cooperative group has or knows it has access to:

☐ *People:*
Who are the committed members of the group? What skills do they have in business, production, sales, or organisation?

Why do they want to be involved?
Who else might be available?
□ *Finance:*
Will the members be able to contribute funds?
Is there any special scheme for grants in your area?
Do you know if you can obtain a loan?
Any other sources (of help in kind as well as money)?
□ *Premises and equipment:*
Are premises available or can they be found?
Are the equipment and machinery to hand?
What else do you know might be available?

When you are looking at your resources it is useful also to consider your commitment in going ahead with planning a business. It will be time-consuming, which has implications for your family, so it is as well that they are enthusiastic about what you are doing. You may have no cash to put in but you will certainly be putting in 'sweat equity' – that is time and effort for which you don't get paid. The objective of any cooperative is to pay decent wages, but it is quite possible that in the struggle to get going wage levels may be one element which gets squeezed. Being part of a co-operative is to share responsibilities and that means worries too which get taken home at night rather than left behind at knocking-off time. An important resource for any cooperative group is the determination to win through and the enthusiasm which can give the commitment to cope with the hard work and the hassle.

Stage 2. Look in detail at your business idea. There are three key questions which must be posed and answered:

□ *Will it sell?* Are you certain that there is a market for what you plan to make or do?
□ *Will it pay?* Can you sell enough at a price sufficient to cover all the costs which will be incurred?

☐ *Can it be done?* Is the idea technically possible and can you find both the machinery/equipment and the people needed to do it?

> The objective is to find a product or a service which will sell at a price sufficient to cover all costs – materials, wages, all running and overhead expenses – and still leave a little over.

Will it sell?

Finding out if you have a market or market research can sound complicated and we look at both marketing and selling in some detail in Chapter 6. Essentially it is a simple matter of assessing whether people will buy what you intend to offer. This can be quite a sophisticated process involving questionnaires, the study of trade and market information and the use of expensive consultants. For most cooperative groups, especially at the start-up stage of a project, it is a more practical process of identifying the market you are aiming at, examining the competition and getting out and asking questions, and seeking commitments from potential customers.

Failing to be certain about the market is a too common cause of small business failure, yet at the end of the day you cannot be quite certain until you actually start trading and selling. There is a moment when you take a deep breath and find out the hard way whether your plans and your market research were right!

If you plan to provide a local service it is more immediately clear whether the service already exists locally and if there will be a demand. A few simple questions and a little observation can establish if there is a potential market. It is often possible to provide the service in a small way at first and so test the market for real, and then build up. If you are planning to invest considerable funds in machinery and equipment and produce a new product, then you need to be much more certain of your market and future sales. That means trying to get advance orders, letters of commitment, survey results which show a very positive interest, comparisons of price and avail- ability which show your product to have an advantage, and so forth. It is essential that you carry out a systematic market study in parallel with researching and developing your product. It can be a costly process both in time and money and for these reasons cooperative groups are likely to look for products which require only low-cost capital investment and for which a market gap is quickly obvious.

Will it pay?

How much will it cost to provide your service or make your product and cover wages, materials, premises, transport, advertising, administration, interest charges, bad debts etc? In turn, how much will you need to charge in order to cover your costs *and* leave some profit over?

Having established the cost, is that cost reasonable? In other words will people buy your service or product at your price or are you in danger of pricing yourself out of the market?

Calculating the costs is not complicated – simply list every cost you can think of (see Stage 3 of the feasibility study process below) – but it can be dis- appointing to discover that there is no way you can carry out your plan and be viable. Too often the idea is possible, the market is there, but the sums add up to too high a price.

Can it be done?

If it is a service you are considering, like hairdressing, electrical repairs, painting and decorating, it is usually clear fairly quickly whether your idea can be carried out. Where a new product is being researched and developed, a key element is not only to ascertain if it can be made but how to manufacture in quantity.

What is usually more difficult is *finding the right people* with the right skills at the right time. The workers' cooperative has to build up a group which includes all the skills needed to run the business. That means not only workers to make the product or provide the service, but people to organise day-to-day schedules, do the selling, handle the administration, keep the books, and plan ahead.

Most community cooperatives start with some management support funded by grant-aid but they set out to create jobs for people who are out of work in areas of high unemployment. In such areas it can be a slow and difficult process to find the right people. Seldom have many local residents had experience of working in or running their own business. The long-term unemployed are more likely to be unskilled – or what skills they have are rusty or outmoded. People who have been out of work for any length of time can find it a hard process getting back into the swing again. All this means going slowly and sometimes building business projects around the skills and interests of one or two key people. It can also mean recruiting some key personnel from outside the specific local area of benefit.

Resources you will need

Having looked at the resources you have available and checked if your business idea will work, you come to *Stage 3* of your feasibility study which is to examine the resources you will need to get the business under way.

People
What particular skills are missing from your group?
How will you set about finding new people?

Finance
Having worked out what you are planning to do and before you start to look for finance, you must calculate how much finance you will need. (Some of this will have been calculated as part of your sums in Stage 2: Will it pay?)

It is useful to prepare three distinct budgets:

47

1. *Pre-start development costs:* what you might have to spend to find out *if* you can start and as part of the planning process.
2. *Pre-start capital costs:* what you must spend *before* you start.
3. *The first year's estimated costs:* the trading costs of the first year (it may be necessary to include cost projections for two or three years).

   (a) *Pre-start development costs*

   Administration: ie, the costs of organising and running your group.

   Market research.

   Feasibility studies.

   Property surveys.

   Legal costs: ie, incorporation of the cooperative or company.

   Recruitment and training of key personnel.

   (b) *Pre-start capital costs*

   Premises: conversion work, fittings.

   Machinery, tools and equipment.

   Transport.

   Office equipment.

   Furniture.

   Initial stocks.

   (c) *Year 1 budget*

   Materials and stock.

   Wages (including national insurance).

   Premises: rent and rates, heat and light, power. Cleaning, repairs and maintenance.

   Sales: transport, packaging, advertising.

   Management: wages (including national insurance), telephone, postage, stationery.

   Finance: bank charges, audit, insurance, interest, bad debts, depreciation, loss/wastage.

Once you have produced your year 1 budget (make sure it is realistic – it is better to over-estimate costs and allow for every conceivable thing rather than find you have under-estimated), you should prepare a *cash flow projection*. This shows when you will have to spend money over a given period and relates it to when you expect to receive money in (see Figure 4). Typically, a lot of money is spent before you start and in the early weeks and months. Income only builds up slowly as you make sales, but wages must be paid each week. You have to pay for stock and materials before you have finished processing and selling them. Often people you have sold to will be slow in paying.

The cash flow projection analyses when you expect certain expenses to be made and how you expect income to flow in. Often more will go out than will come in and it will take time for the income flow to accumulate and exceed the early extra outgoings. The difference between what is going out and what is coming in shows you how much money you have to have from time to time to remain solvent: that is your *working capital*.

	Pre-start	Week 1	Week 2	Week 3	Week 4	Week 5
Expenditure:						
Stock	3,000	2,000	—	—	2,000	—
Costs	15,000	1,500	1,500	1,500	2,000	2,000
Income:						
Grant/loan	20,000	—	—	—	—	—
Sales	—	—	500	1,250	3,000	3,500
Balance[1]	2,000	(3,500)	(1,000)	(250)	(1,000)	1,500
Cumulative balance (deficit)[2]	2,000	(1,500)	(2,500)	(2,750)	(3,750)	(2,250)

1. The balance is the difference between income and expenditure for that particular period.

2. The cumulative balance is the actual money you have (or do not have) and shows how much money you will need to obtain (by bank overdraft, for example) simply to keep going.

4. Cash flow

So the funds you need are:
    Pre-start development finance.
    Initial capital.
    Working capital.

Your financial budget and cash flow projection does more than tell you what you need, it acts as a model plan for your business against which to compare what actually happens. If the income does not flow in as you anticipate, why not? Has something gone wrong? If your expenditure is greater than expected, why?

Premises and equipment
How much space do you require?
Where do you want to be located?
Is all the machinery and equipment you require available, and what are delivery dates like?

Business plan
With all the feasibility study homework complete, you can now prepare a business plan. This acts as the basic document you will use to raise finance for your project. The contents of a business plan are described in Chapter 4, but preparing the plan is also an important process for the cooperative group as it sets down what you intend to do. If the plan has been jointly prepared and agreed then it will be a sound foundation on which to develop as well as a yardstick against which to measure progress. For this reason it is important that the members of the intending cooperative understand the plan. Accountants, cooperative development officers and others can help you put it together, but it is *your* plan. Make sure you understand it.

Chapter 4

Raising Finance

Finding finance for a new cooperative enterprise is often wrongly thought of as the first and main problem and that can dissuade groups from even thinking about setting up on their own, but looking for finance comes *after* you have got together and sorted out your idea and the people. Once you know *what* you are going to do, *how* you are going to do it, *who* is going to do it and that it appears to be *viable*, then you are ready to start seeking funds.

A group with a well thought-out plan and the obvious competence to carry it out stands a good chance of raising whatever finance is needed, although it may take time and patience. A half-baked idea, a bad plan, and a lack of skills and commitment from the people concerned will stand no chance of getting financial support.

Problems

The problems which are special to cooperatives when they are seeking finance – especially start-up finance – from normal commercial sources include:

1. The financial structure of most cooperatives is based on a nominal shareholding or minimal guarantee on the principle that ownership and control remain with the work-force or within the local community (see Chapter 7). For this reason, there is no opportunity for equity investment in the cooperative which is the usual method of obtaining high risk investment.
2. Cooperatives are often started by groups of workers or local residents who have little or no capital resources of their own to put into the

51

business or offer as security to potential lenders. They are investing their skills, labour and effort in the cooperative enterprise rather than finance.

3. Lack of capital and personal security can disqualify cooperatives from obtaining loans from public agencies and commercial sources which usually demand some evidence of financial contribution by the launching members.

4. Often only modest loans tend to be requested by cooperatives and many lending institutions are simply not geared to making small loans. Indeed, most find it unprofitable to administer them.

5. A fundamental cooperative principle is that there should be a limited rate of return on capital compared with benefit to the members. This can make it legally difficult for cooperatives to accept high interest loans.

6. Banks and other lending institutions often have misconceptions about cooperatives. They include doubts about the limited liability of cooperatives, the belief that they lack efficient management, organisational and decision-making structures, and seeing cooperatives as charitable organisations rather than the viable business enterprises they set out to be.

This last point is especially pertinent to community cooperatives which emphasise their commitment to both social and commercial objectives and which in some instances have been granted charitable status while remaining essentially business enterprises.

Specialist sources of finance

There are now sources of finance specially geared to the needs of both worker cooperatives and community cooperatives.

1. Industrial Common Ownership Finance Ltd (ICOF)

ICOF was set up in 1973 as a revolving loan fund especially for worker cooperatives. It is a company limited by guarantee whose members are also members of the Industrial Common Ownership Movement. The company is managed by a board of ten trustees and run by a small executive based in Northampton.

ICOF funds for lending have come from three principal sources: £220,000 allocated by the Department of Industry; loan finance provided by the Scott Bader Commonwealth from an allocation of that company's profits; and contributions from organisations and individuals wishing to support the growth of workers' cooperatives.

During 1982 ICOF agreed with the West Midlands County Council to establish a loan fund exclusively for worker cooperatives in the West Midland county area and the County Council has granted £325,000 into that fund. It is hoped to repeat this arrangement with other local authorities throughout Britain.

The ICOF central fund amounted to £240,000 in June 1983. There were 33 worker cooperatives in receipt of loan finance from the central fund and 16 from the West Midlands fund after eight months. Most ICOF borrowers are small start-up cooperatives and approval of an ICOF loan has frequently been the first step in helping a cooperative group to put together a financial package and encourage other lenders, such as the bank and the local authority, to join in. Most ICOF loans are small (in the region of £2,500 to £10,000) and medium term (repayable over five years).

Grassroots Bookshop

Grassroots was set up as a partnership in Manchester specialising in radical and left-wing books. At the time of converting into a cooperative in 1977 the business ran two shops and had built up a turnover of some £60,000. They applied for and received a loan from

ICOF to help with working capital. By this time two key business questions had emerged: could the business sustain two shops, and could the business build up enough sales to be profitable by just selling to its specialised market, or should it widen the range of its stock and so appeal to a wider range of customers?

The first question was fairly easily decided and the shop near the university was closed leaving just the city centre site. The question of stock range and target customer group caused more heartache. Eventually the business broadened out from their original radical, left-wing focus, but without sacrificing that part of their business which was, after all, their original purpose.

Profitability has since risen regularly and the 1982 turnover increased to £300,000. The ICOF loan was fully repaid by December 1981. Grassroots now have a solid reputation not only as a bookshop but as a cooperative bookshop which is willing to advise and assist other new cooperatives struggling to set up.

There have been changes in the membership. In 1978 there were two women and five men, in 1983 five women and two men. Some former worker members have remained active in the cooperative movement either setting up other bookshops or moving to become cooperative development workers.

Fiddington Fixings

In 1980 it was announced that a small factory in Fiddington, part of a much larger group, was being closed down so that the factory site could be sold for a substantial sum. Production of the specialised fixing made at the factory was to be phased out and the Fiddington workers made redundant. A group of 12 shop-floor workers and the production manager decided to try and keep in business and form a cooperative. The main customer for the fixing indicated that they would buy from the cooperative provided that the fixing remained technically up to standard. That order guaranteed at least 12 months' production.

Each of the cooperative members contributed £1,000 from their redundancy payments. The parent company cooperated in selling plant and machinery on reasonable terms. There was substantial support from the local authority which was very committed to helping the cooperative, and found premises for it. A business plan was prepared which indicated potential viability and profitability, and on the basis of the plan a funding package was arranged with the national cooperative loan fund and their bank. The cooperative was a production business and had no in-house management or sales expertise. To compensate for this lack a business adviser was appointed.

Production started and thousands of fixings were manufactured. The first batch sent to the customer was returned with queries about the specifications and the quality. While discussions were held, production continued. The discussions with the customer finally uncovered the fact that what had been taken as a letter of *intent* was only a letter of *interest*. The customer did not actually want the fixings.

Four months after the cooperative started trading it became very apparent that there was no market for the fixings. Substantial debts had been built up and all the money invested was lost. Although the potential customer could be said to have a moral obligation to buy from the cooperative, there was no legal obligation. The cooperative was consequently liquidated.

2. Local authority schemes

(*a*) The West Midlands loan fund for worker cooperatives has been created by paying a grant to ICOF who administers it (see page 53).

(*b*) Other local authorities (notably Sheffield and the City of Glasgow District Council) have arranged to guarantee loans which might be made by a bank to worker cooperatives in their area. In the Sheffield scheme loans are made within the context of an 'employment agreement' which reflects the council's views about socially useful production, seeks acceptable rates of pay and conditions for workers and attempts to ascertain the level of employment likely to be created.

(*c*) The Inner Urban Areas Act 1978 gives designated district councils the power to make grants of up to £1,000 to intending cooperative groups towards the costs of planning and incorporating their enterprise.

(*d*) The urban aid programme has been used extensively by local authorities to fund the staff costs of local cooperative development agencies. Urban aid is available in areas of special need and deprivation and is processed via the local authority to central government, with central government paying 75 per cent of the approved grant.

(*e*) The urban aid programme has been used also (notably in Strathclyde Region) to fund the provision of basic business management and administrative personnel for community cooperatives during their crucial first three to five years of establishment and development. In some cases urban aid grant has also financed the conversion of premises (for example, to provide workshops) and the provision of equipment. It has not been available to provide working capital for day-to-day trading activites.

Strathclyde Region expects to create a Community Business Development Unit in April 1984 which will provide a 'one-door' structure for giving community cooperative development advice and support *and* for providing finance.[1]

3. Highlands and Islands Development Board (HIDB)

In 1977 the HIDB announced a special programme of support and funding for community cooperatives, modelled on experience gained in the west of Ireland, and first targeted at the Western Isles, although it has since been extended to all the Highlands and Islands.

The community cooperative programme has consisted of four main elements:

Field officers, whose job has been both to explain the programme to local communities and to work with local steering groups, helping them to develop their plans for establishing a community cooperative in their locality.

Establishment grants matching pound for pound funds raised by the local steering group up to £20,000 and so helping to give the cooperative enterprise some of its own capital, some equity.

---

1. *Strathclyde Digest*, No 37; Strathclyde Regional Council 17 August 1983.

Management grants to pay for the costs of a manager and back-up administration at the rate of 100 per cent for three years and 50 per cent for years four and five.

Access to the usual loan and grant schemes which the HIDB has as part of its usual work of encouraging development generally in the Highlands and Islands.

As a consequence of establishing this pioneering scheme a dozen community cooperatives have been set up in remote communities. The results of this programme are now being assessed.

4. Development Board for Rural Wales
Mid Wales Development also has an experimental support scheme for community cooperatives. For a cooperative involved in both community development and employment creation this includes meeting 50 per cent of the cost of a manager for the first three years.

5. Industry
As the recession has deepened, industry has increasingly shown an interest in supporting local economic self-help initiatives. Support comes in four ways: advice, cash, secondment of personnel and the gift of goods and equipment. Whereas advice can be fairly readily available to all forms of new enterprise, through such agencies as Local Enterprise Trusts, the other forms of assistance are more usually reserved for community cooperatives which are committed to distribute profits only for community benefit. The Action Resource Centre and Business in the Community Organisations are committed to assist community-based employment initiatives (see Appendix 1 for further details). Shell UK, National Westminster Bank, IBM, Levi Strauss and other companies have a record of positive and practical assistance towards community cooperatives.

57

Levi Strauss and Co
Special Emphasis Grants Scheme

As from 1 January 1983, the Special Emphasis Grants in the Northern Europe Division will only be given for the purposes of *community-based local economic developments*.

In particular we are concerned to stimulate and support the development of training and employment initiatives which will strengthen and diversify the local economic structure of our plant communities. Specifically the company is seeking to promote community-based projects and enterprises which lead to the creation of long-term jobs by providing socially useful goods and services on a self-financing basis.

This programme is centred on the United Kingdom where our plants tend to be located in areas of high and prolonged unemployment and the experience of the past two years has led us to believe that we can play a useful role in stimulating local economic initiatives of a self-help type. We look forward to furthering this work in partnership with public, private and community-based organisations.

Other sources of finance

For many cooperative groups there is no special funding to which they have immediate access; it is necessary for them to explore systematically all possible sources of finance in order to pull together a package to suit their needs. Even for groups with access to one of the special arrangements, these seldom provide for all the finance required and it is equally important to look at the range of other sources.

1. Banks
The High Street bank is likely to be the first source of ordinary commercial finance to be tapped by a cooperative. Bank finance might come either as an overdraft up to an agreed amount usually for working capital or as a medium-term loan for the fixed assets of the business (ie, some particular item of equipment or machinery). The bank's decision will be made partly on 'track record' which makes it difficult for the starting-up

cooperative, and on available security, also a difficult condition for the starting-up cooperative to meet.

It is important to remember that the main job of the bank is to safeguard its depositors' money. From this comes the essential caution of the bank manager. All managers are entitled to make loan decisions up to a certain ceiling without referring a case to someone else: in general, the smaller the branch the lower the manager's ceiling. In 1978 the Cooperative Bank announced a loan scheme for workers' cooperatives which lends up to £25,000 on a pound for pound ratio to funds committed to the enterprise by the worker members themselves. In practice most banks will do the same, given that they think the proposal stands a reasonable chance of success.

When multi-purpose community cooperatives are involved in more than one activity, it is usual for a bank to require the specific business activity to which it is being asked to lend to be constituted as a separate legal entity (see Chapter 6).

2. Members and resources

All cooperatives depend on the 'sweat equity' of their members to get off the ground and that demonstrable commitment from members can also elicit support from other people and agencies. Likewise some form of financial contribution can both help capitalise the project at the start and further demonstrate members' commitment and determination.

☐ Membership subscriptions or cooperative share-holdings can be used both to extend membership and raise funds. Some of the HIDB community cooperatives have raised several thousand pounds in this way from community members and expatriates.
☐ Local fund-raising activities can contribute valuable finance in the early days, especially for community cooperatives.
☐ Members of the cooperative might either

contribute or lend (at low interest rates or none) personal funds to the business. This is an increasingly common means of initially funding a workers' cooperative – especially one where workers have received redundancy payments – and it provides a base of 'own capital' on which can be built a package of other finance.

☐ Working without wages or for low pay is also a way of workers capitalising the business. The rules surrounding employment and supplementary benefits make it very difficult for people to trade while still in receipt of benefit which makes working for no wages a rare occurrence. However, the members of many cooperative groups make some kind of financial sacrifice either through accepting relatively low wages while the business establishes itself or by signing on and off the dole with the ebb and flow of work.

3. Enterprise Allowance

The Department of Employment has established the enterprise allowance scheme which pays a basic £40 per week allowance for 12 months to people attempting to set up their own self-employment business. The two main conditions are that the person has been previously unemployed for 13 weeks and that they are putting £1,000 into the business. This scheme effectively allows people on unemployment or supplementary benefit to take the step into self-employment knowing that for the first 52 weeks they will have a guaranteed income of £40 per week regardless of how their business goes.

There has been some flexibility in how the £1,000 is made up, materials and equipment having been counted as well as cash, provided they have been purchased after applying for an allowance, and the scheme has been available to worker cooperative enterprises numbering not more than ten members. It has not yet been agreed that the scheme can be used in the same way by community cooperatives as the workers there do not work for themselves.

4. Manpower Services Commission

None of the MSC special programmes is designed for helping people create viable, commercial business enterprises. They are intended to provide the chance of some work of community benefit for one year at most for people who have been out of work for more than six months.

Despite the rules and regulations some community cooperatives have used an MSC funded project either to test out a potential business idea or to provide a training period for a group of workers. While this can and has been done it is not a satisfactory arrangement as the object of an MSC scheme is to generate numbers of temporary jobs and that conflicts with the community cooperative's objective of setting up a commercially viable enterprise. Furthermore, when an MSC supported scheme does trade, any income it generates must be offset against future grant and may not be used to accumulate working capital.

Flagstone Enterprises

Flagstone Enterprises is a community company based in Ferguslie Park, a council housing estate on the outskirts of Paisley in the west of Scotland. The area has always had an unemployment rate between two and three times the national average and has been known for a high incidence of other social, community and family problems many of which arise from unemployment and low incomes. The area also has a strong tradition of community self-help and action. In the mid-70s, the local tenants' organisation, together with locally based community workers, set up a joinery workers' cooperative using the MSC's Job Creation Programme. The cooperative did not long survive after grant aid ended, but the experience strengthened a local determination to try and do something to create jobs locally.

In 1979 the tenants' association, with assistance from the Local Enterprise Advisory Project, planned a community company based initially around the previous stone-cleaning experience of the vice-chairman. Support was obtained from the MSC for a one-year graffiti removal project on public buildings and from the urban programme to pay for a manager and administrative costs. In the first year of operation, 1980–81, the company did non-commercial graffiti removal work and built up a competent stone-cleaning squad. The company also explored other areas of work: general contracting, car breaking, printing, retailing 'fancy goods' and producing a royal wedding souvenir.

None of these other activities – apart from general contracting for erratic periods of time – proved profitable and by the end of the MSC grant year the company found itself with a proven ability to stone-clean but without adequate contracts to make a smooth transition from grant-aided graffiti removal to commercial stone-cleaning.

For nine months a new manager worked hard to build up orders and was backed up by a small group of key workers who were prepared to sign on and off the dole as work was available in order to help build up the company. One year later that key group were in regular work and Flagstone Enterprises was becoming known as a competent and competitive stone-cleaning and stone-restoration company.

By the summer of 1983 after three years of management grant from the urban programme the company had built up its labour force to over 30 and was working on up to six contracts at a time. At this point, with a further two years of management grant available, the company was able to start looking again at other areas of work which would create jobs for un-employed, and usually unskilled, people of Ferguslie Park.

Under the new Community Programme, it is possible for a group of part-time workers to start developing a business enterprise in the time when they are *not* working on the Community Programme. In this way their CP work can give them some wages to live on while they build up their own or community business in their own time, and as they are *waged* rather than in receipt of benefit they do not lose income as a consequence of earning except through income tax at the standard rate if they earn enough (see Chapter 5).

Some community cooperatives have found it useful to sponsor and run MSC supported schemes simply as one way of doing something practical in their community while they set about the hard and slow slog of planning and raising finance for their actual business activities.

5. Local sources

Friends or relations can assist either by providing a loan or by giving a guarantee against which a loan from elsewhere can be secured. However, if private capital assistance is obtained in this way it is important to make a properly drawn up agreement so that the lender and the cooperative group know where they stand. There is nothing worse than friendships or family relationships soured by a later misunderstanding over money.

Local organisations - such as trade unions, churches, Rotary, sports clubs etc - can often be persuaded to contribute funds to a group of workers or residents who are trying to save or create jobs in the locality. The community benefit angle can be used especially by community cooperatives and there is often a considerable fund of local goodwill which can be turned into money or goods and equipment. As well as local organisations, business people will sometimes help and it might be worth tracking down former residents who have since become wealthy or famous (or both!).

In some areas there are special local trusts which benefit a particular area only. District Councils and Councils of Social Service (Voluntary Service Councils or Rural Community Councils in some areas) usually hold information about such trust funds. Most local libraries will have a reference copy of the *Directory of Grant-Making Trusts*.

6. Central government assistance

Certain parts of the country are designated assisted areas (Special Development Areas, Development Areas and Intermediate Areas) where new business development can qualify for a range of assistance. This includes regional development grants for buildings and new machinery (22 per cent), loans, interest relief grants and removal grants, rent-free periods in advance factories, various help for transferred workers and special depreciation and tax allowances. Assistance available is well summarised in the Department of Industry booklet *Incentives for Industry in the Areas for Expansion*. The first step for any intending cooperative group is to find out what assistance may be available in their area and second, if it will be applicable to them. Too often start-up cooperative groups are too small for the central government assistance schemes or are setting up in the service sector which generally does not qualify. There are regional offices of the Department of Industry; most county and regional local authorities (and indeed districts) will provide this information.

A government-backed *loan guarantee scheme* was started in June 1981 involving 30 banks and financial institutions. The Department of Industry will guarantee 80 per cent of medium-term loans (from two to seven years) and for this guarantee an extra 3 per cent is added to the interest rate. The intention is to encourage banks to make some loans when they ordinarily might not take the risk, but the higher interest rate can make this very expensive money.

7. Regional agencies

In Scotland there are two regional development agencies: the Highlands and Islands Development Board and the Scottish Development Agency. The Welsh Development Agency, the Development Board for Rural Wales (Mid Wales Development) and the Council for Small Industries in Rural Areas (in England) have powers to make loans, provide factory space and offer marketing, management, financial and technical assistance.

The Scottish Development Agency special project agreement with the Scottish Cooperatives Development Committee aids the promotion of worker cooperatives but does not make special provision for financing them. The SDA has, however, been setting up special projects in certain high unemployment areas in which reference is now being made to community cooperatives and providing modest financial assistance both for researching business ideas and for providing working capital.

Denny Bonnybridge Project

Financial assistance will be provided to existing and new community business to help with development ideas. Assistance will take the form of:

(a) Grants and loans for development of business ideas and business plans, market studies and market development (up to £30,000 in total).

(b) Grants and loans for working capital on a matching £ for £ basis (up to £20,000 in total).

From the SDA's project agreement June 1983

---

8. Local authorities

In addition to the financial schemes above, local authorities generally can provide premises for business use and increasingly have a number of redundant buildings such as schools which can be used. Cooperative groups are often allocated such premises at nil or peppercorn rent.

In addition some local authorities have established special local small business loan and grant funds which can be used to develop new business enterprises. Others have created special employment subsidy schemes which can pay, for example, 30 per cent of the wages for the first six months of any new job which is filled by someone who has been unemployed for six months or longer. (For small firms – less than 25 employees – the six-month rule can be waived.)[2]

Different local authorities – regional, county and district – have different schemes, priorities and policies. It is important to make contact with your local councils to find out what they might do to help you both financially and otherwise.

---

2. Strathclyde Region leaflet *Employment Grants Scheme 1983/84.*

9. Deferred payments

One means of reducing the amount of money your cooperative requires is to defer certain payments. This can be done in two ways:

1. Obtaining credit: by buying materials and stock on credit you might have some income flowing in before you have to pay your supplier. This can be a double-edged tactic, however, if your customers start delaying their payments to you!
2. Obtaining equipment or machinery on HP or lease rather than buying. It is important to look carefully into the full implications of entering into such an arrangement and to beware of unduly high interest charges.

Preparing a business prospectus

When you apply for money it is important to present your case clearly. In sorting out the feasibility of your idea you should have prepared a basic business plan and forecast. To make an application for funds you want to dress that business plan up into a detailed package which includes the following sections:

1. *About the cooperative:* explain who are the members of the cooperative and how it came to be formed; explain exactly the legal structure adopted and the objectives of the cooperative. (For banks and most official bodies you will also have to attach a copy of your legal constitution.)
2. *About the idea:* describe exactly what it is you plan to do and demonstrate that it can be done. Show that you realise what skills are required and that you have the people with them. Show also that you can obtain whatever machinery, equipment and raw materials that might be needed.
3. *About the market:* demonstrate that you have done your market research and present the evidence that a market does exist for your product or service. Explain your costings and

show that your price is both realistic and properly competitive. Explain your sales targets.

4. *About your organisation:* explain how your company will be organised and managed and that you have made certain you have in the business or available to it the marketing, selling and management skills as well as the production ability. Remember that the very idea of a worker or community cooperative will make some people expect inefficiency and an unbusinesslike approach. Explain what financial control systems you are setting up.

5. *About finance:* show what funds the business already has and explain how much finance is needed before you start, in order to start and as working capital once you have begun. Show by means of a cash flow projection how your anticipated income relates to your planned expenditure and when you expect your business to become profitable. If your cooperative already has a track record of some trading activity provide the evidence of past accounts to demonstrate your proven ability.

6. *About support:* show who you have consulted about your plans, also what sources of support and advice you have access to.

Presenting your package

It is important to present your business prospectus as well as possible. Try and ensure that it looks good in terms of layout, standard of typing and photocopies etc. Photographs and diagrams can make descriptions more vivid and the plan more attractive to read. Remember that the main purpose of your prospectus is to win support which means persuading people that you have done your preparation thoroughly and that you are worth backing.

Your prospectus will sometimes be the first impression of the proposal to reach a prospective backer. First impressions are important so give careful thought to wording the letter, how you will deal with the telephone call to arrange an appointment to discuss the matter, and to how your representatives appear when they turn up for that first appointment.

For all the systematic care and calculation put into the preparation and presentation of your business package, the final decision often depends on human feeling that an idea in the hands of a particular group will work. That human element in decision-making is important, and since backing a business is to back people, you must carry conviction that you can make a success of your plan. It also means that a refusal of support from one quarter may change to agreement to back you in another. If you believe your plan is good, don't let a 'No' put you off. Go and try and persuade someone else!

Chapter 5
Money and Financial Control

The two essential money matters of running any enterprise are first, to keep adequate and up-to-date accounting records so that you can keep track of all the money passing in and out of your business and second, to use this financial information to tell you how your business is doing at any time.

Financial information and control

Financial control must be held by the people in the cooperative enterprise. It is not enough to produce boxes of paper for the accountant to take away once or twice a year and come back to tell you if you are profitable or not. Financial control is a question of keeping the business on course: checking actual progress and outcome against the plan.

Cooperatives have a variety of management structures and styles but there must always be someone designated to keep an eye on the enterprise's health and use the information available about regular financial transactions to control and assess progress. It is also important that other members of the cooperative understand both the importance of producing financial information and how it can be used. There should be nothing mysterious or difficult about financial data.

There are three questions which are central to the business of financial control:

☐ Are we meeting our targets?
☐ Are we profitable?
☐ Do we have enough cash?

Targets
When drawing up the business plan, your cooperative group will have fixed certain targets. As you monitor actual performance against the plan you will be regularly adjusting the targets in the light of real experience. The main targets for your business will concern sales, production and costs. Failure to meet them gives an immediate warning that things are not going according to plan and that you must consider remedial action.

Sales
Your plan established the minimum sales you must make in order to break even. If you are not achieving these sales, why not? Are there special seasonal trends? Should you reduce your price? Are your sales people not getting to the right places? Do you need to improve your advertising? Have you misjudged the target market? Is there something wrong with your product?

Production
Are you producing the quantity you planned in the time scheduled? Are you doing as much work as you intended? In other words, is the production or service cost what you intended? Is the quality of your product or service as high as you first expected? Are there any ways of making improvements or cutting costs? Did you correctly estimate the size of work-force needed for your planned output?

Costs
Your annual budget estimated the various overheads. Are your estimates correct? Has the cost of materials changed? Has there been any unexpected expenditure? Are such items as phone calls, transport, postage etc within budget?

It might be helpful to prepare a break-even chart which shows at what point your output/sales are earning enough income/revenue to cover your fixed overhead costs and start making a profit.

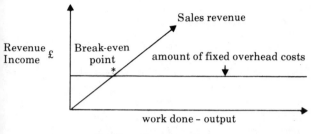

5. Break-even chart

The variable costs directly related to production or service will be recovered automatically as your output increases if your pricing is right, but the basic overhead costs of running the enterprise are virtually the same whether your output is small or large.

Other factors which can significantly affect performance and which your plant should have made some notional allowance for are:

Sickness. Time off through sickness is working time lost to the enterprise; statutory sick pay is money paid out and lost to the business until claimed back from the government.

Staff turnover. Like any other business, cooperatives have a turnover of workers: people may not fit in, leave the district, go for another job. The effect on the enterpise is to reduce performance until a new worker is recruited and fitted in.

Wastage. Although any plan will allow for wastage and loss, this can be a much bigger factor than bargained for. Mistakes can be made all too easily and flawed production which has to be sold cheaply or even scrapped can completely upset the best laid plans and targets.

Debts. Any plan must allow for some bad debts, but too many small businesses are themselves pulled down simply because one customer fails and goes into liquidation leaving accounts unpaid. The only (partial) safeguard is to try and build up a good cross section of customers, but for the small co-

71

operative one seemingly good large customer is an almost irresistible attraction.

Financial control is therefore about monitoring performance in relation to the original business plan and any subsequent adjustments to specific targets. Week by week, month by month, the cooperative should know how it is doing. All members should at least appreciate the significance of the sales achieved in relation to the costs and time of production and expenses of running the business.

Remedial action, if performance does not match targets, focuses on three areas:

☐ Increase sales.
☐ Reduce costs.
☐ Conserve cash.

Conserving cash only puts off the day of reckoning if the basic problem is one of unprofitability: that is if you cannot sell enough of what you are offering at a price which is adequate to meet all costs and leave something over.

Cash

Having enough cash (often called liquidity) is probably the biggest financial problem facing any small enterprise. It is possible to be profitable but still to run out of cash for paying the bills as they come in. A cash shortage is usually caused when you have to pay out for material or equipment a long time before it produces income. While you are working to turn it into income there are all the regular bills to be met. It can be especially frustrating for a small business when it is building up to have to *turn down* a big order because it cannot find the cash to finance it! Yet overtrading – taking on more than you can cope with – is a very common cause of problems and indeed failure. If you take the big order, buy the materials, employ the extra staff – can you pay for it all before the payments start to flow in?

Your *cash flow* forecast is the main means of

monitoring the cash position and will have been prepared as part of the business planning process (see page 48). The cash flow assesses your cash receipts in a given period (month, quarter, year) and the payments to be made, resulting in either a positive (surplus) or a negative (deficit) cash figure. When assessing the cash situation great care must be taken over the timing of the flows in and out. Sales may be made in one month but you may not receive the cash until two or three months later, and the same can apply to payments you have to make.

It is helpful to think of the cash requirement (working capital) in terms of a cycle: materials and stock must be purchased and this is a cash outflow. Only when the goods are sold do we start to see a cash inflow. It is in the business's interest to speed up the cycle and so realise the surplus being created: to produce, sell and receive payment as quickly as possible, while at the same time delaying as far as is sensible the outflow of money to suppliers.

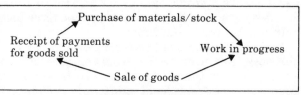

6. Cash requirement

The cycle can be speeded up by:

(a) Invoicing as quickly as possible after a sale is made.
(b) Offering discounts for quick payments.
(c) Delaying payments for goods received as far as this is practical or indeed reasonable; obviously it is unwise to delay payment to the extent that it risks legal action or incurs the wrath of suppliers. It is possible to find out the 'normal' ratio of debts to sales for different types of industry and business and this

debtors' ratio can give a shorthand measure of how well the money is coming in.

Accounting records

In order for a cooperative to exert the sort of financial control described it is vital that proper records are kept up to date. There are three golden rules:

1. All transactions must be written down: do not trust to memory.
2. Invoices, vouchers and receipts should be kept for all money transactions.
3. All cash should, where possible, go through the bank account(s).

The purpose of your book-keeping system is (a) to record the money transactions in your business from day to day and (b) provide the information to monitor your performance. Book-keeping and other record systems should be as simple as possible. Too often they appear complicated, in part because many people do not find figures easy but also because a jargon and mystique have been built up around accountancy.

When setting up a book-keeping system for your business, take advice either from your accountant, an officer from the local cooperative development agency, or from your local industrial development unit. What you are after is a system which suits what you are doing and one which you can understand and operate easily. If you don't understand anything, keep asking until you do! Do not, however, try and re-invent the wheel. Many tried and tested basic systems of book-keeping exist and ready-made books and accounting stationery can be purchased from most reputable stationers.

The minimum of book-keeping requirements of any business will consist of:

Cash book
All money received, by cheque or cash, and all payments through the bank (that is by cheque)

should be entered in the cash book. This is the central record of income and expenditure. For every item of expenditure there should be a voucher – some form of receipt or account or other form of explanation. Vouchers should be filed in the order in which their items appear in the cash book. See Figures 7 and 8. (Note the headings of the columns in the cash book and the number of columns are chosen to suit the needs of the particular cooperative.)

Date	Detail	Bankings	Sales/ Takings	Other
July 1	Takings	400	400	
July 2	Takings		260	
	Council grant instalment	5,260		5,000
July 3	Takings	300	300	
July 4	Takings	330	330	
July 5	ICOF loan			4,500
	Takings	4,780	280	

7. Cash book: Receipts . . .

Petty cash book

All businesses need some cash in hand for small purchases which require cash rather than a cheque. A petty cash account is started for this purpose. Usually it is simply cash in a box and the cash comes by way of a cheque made out to cash which has been entered in the cash book as a payment. (Sometimes a petty cash bank account is opened into which the cheque is paid.) All cash payments are recorded in the petty cash book and for each there should be a voucher. (For some small expenses there may be no receipt, in which case the person concerned should make up and sign a petty cash voucher.) The only income into the petty cash will be by a cheque made out to cash from the cash book. Normally no sales or other income is paid into petty cash or entered into the petty cash book. It is usual for the petty cash to have an agreed amount of money (a 'float') which is then topped up

Date	Detail	Ref No	Cheque No	Total	VAT	Stock, Materials	Wages N.I.	Rent Rates	Heat, Light Cleaning	Transport	Admin	Misc
July 1	Jones Co	41	068287	334.53	43.63	290.90						
	Westfield Garage	42	288	127.36	16.61					110.75		
	British Telecom	43	289	276.46	36.06						240.40	
	Petty cash	44	290	50.00								50.00
July 2	Wages	45	291	330.00			330.00					
	Fairfield Printers	46	292	85.10	11.10						74.00	
	Lion Cross Insurance	47	293	68.00								68.00
July 3	VPP Oils	48	294	333.78	43.53				290.20			
	Essex Supplies	49	295	541.36	70.61	470.75						
	Inland Revenue June	50	296	446.00			446.00					
	Platwell District Council	51	297	100.00				100.00				

8. . . . and Payments

9. Petty cash book

In	Date	Detail	Ref No	Out Total	VAT	Admin	Cleaning	Transport	Staff	Post	Misc
50.00	July 1	Cheque for cash									
	July 1	Stamps	1	9.00						9.00	
		Menzies: envelopes	2	1.38	0.18	1.20					
	July 2	J Smith: bus fares	3	0.60				0.60			
	July 5	Coffee, milk, sugar	4	1.72					1.72		
		Coop: polish, Domestos	5	2.22	0.29		1.93				
	July 6	Stamps	6	4.22						4.22	
		Coop: string	7	1.50	0.20						1.30
		I Ladd: bus fare	8	0.60				0.60			
		petrol and oil	9	10.95	1.43			9.52			
				32.19							
		Balance in hand		17.81							
				32.19	2.10	1.20	1.93	10.72	1.72	13.22	1.30
50.00				50.00							
17.81	July 8	Balance in hand									
32.19		Cash from bank									
		G McBeth: bus fare	10	0.60				0.60			
	July 9	Coop: milk, sugar	11	0.69					0.69		

10. Purchase ledger

Date	Supplier	Total	VAT Incl	Invoice Received	Payment Due	Payment Made: Date	Cheque No
June 1	Jones Co	334.53	43.63	June 7	June 30	July 1	287
June 4	Fairfield	85.10	11.10	June 15	June 30	July 2	292
June 15	VPP Oils	333.78	43.53	June 20	July 13	July 3	294
June 16	Middgate Ltd	108.79	14.19	July 3	July 31		
June 17	Strathvee	187.34	24.44	July 3	July 31		

each week or month by the amount which has been spent.

Purchase ledger

When your cooperative is buying on credit, it is important to keep a record of what you have ordered and bought, but not yet paid for. You then know what you are commited to paying out. It is only when you actually do pay that you make an entry in the cash book. Each supplier's invoice should be listed in chronological order showing the total sum owing with the VAT amount indicated.

Sales ledger

It is important to keep a record of all sales which you make on credit, so you know what income to expect and who owes you how much. It is only when you actually receive payment that you enter the sale in the cash book.

Date	Customer	Amount Due Total	VAT Incl	Invoice No	Payment Due	Payment Rec
June 1	Lothario Bros	424.60	55.35	3074	June 30	July 2
June 4	Smith & Son	69.80	9.15	3079	June 30	July 3
June 10	Awars Ltd	90.90	11.85	3084	July 15	
June 15	Liddell & Co	106.24	13.80	3094	July 15	

11. Sales ledger

Book-keeping systems do not look after themselves: they have to be kept up and that means making the time available to write up the entries and do the paperwork. It is all too easy to give the book-keeping a low priority and leave it for a spare moment. That way trusts too much to memory and overlooks the fact that spare moments in a small business are for taking a well-earned rest rather than book-keeping. It is an important task essential to running the business and time must accordingly be allocated to it. The better your book-keeping the quicker your accountant can prepare your year-end accounts and the cheaper his audit fee will be.

Profit and loss

With the information contained in the books the cooperative can match its performance to its targets and keep track of its cash position. It is also possible to calculate whether your business is profitable or not. Calculating profit or loss means doing the 'business sum': taking what you have earned by sales in a given period and seeing if it more than covers the total costs of making the goods, making the sales and generally running the business. If it more than covers the costs, then you have made a profit; if not, you have made a loss.

When you take a given period (a month, a quarter, a year) over which to calculate your profit or loss there are bound to be transactions at the beginning and end of the period which overlap with the period before or after. It is, therefore, necessary to make certain adjustments in order to isolate the given period and give an accurate picture. For example, if you started trading in June with a stock of 500 articles already made up and paid for and sold them all in June, your profit calculation for the month must allow for the fact that the cost of materials and production had already been paid for. If you did not make this allowance your 'profit' would appear to be much greater than it actually was.

The 'business sum': the trading profit and loss account

First, calculate the total value of the *sales* made during the given period for which you are working out your profitability. This will consist of sales for which you have received cash and credit sales for which you are still awaiting payment. This total will exclude VAT.

Second, calculate the total of the *direct costs* of making the goods (or providing the services) you have sold (exclusive of VAT). This usually means

		£
1. *Sales*		
Cash		25,000
Credit		10,000
Total sales income		35,000

2. *Direct costs of sales*	£	
Stock in hand at beginning	5,000	
Add: purchases	10,000	
	15,000	
Subtract: stock at end	6,000	
	9,000	
Wages (productive)	10,000	
Total direct costs	19,000	19,000

3. *Gross profit*		16,000

4. *Overhead costs of running the business*		
Premises	1,500	
Transport	2,500	
Advertising	450	
Packaging	400	
Management/sales/admin/ wages	2,850	
Administration	550	
Insurance	250	
Financial charges	200	
Bad debts/wastage	500	
Depreciation	1,200	
	10,400	10,400

5. *Net profit (loss)*		£5,600

12. *The 'business sum': the trading profit and loss account*

the materials and stock you have purchased and the wages of all workers directly engaged in making the product or providing the service. To work out the cost of materials used in the period you take the value you had in hand at the beginning of the period, add to it what you have spent on materials during the period and then subtract the cost value of what is left at the end. You also include in your materials and stock figure any accumulated finished but unsold goods.

Third, by subtracting the total of the direct costs from the sales income we arrive at the *gross profit*. It is this amount which must cover the other costs of running the business (and indeed developing it).

Fourth, calculate the *overhead costs* of running the business during the period under review. These are the costs to do with premises, management and organisation, transport and advertising, depreciation and financial charges and will have been worked out in your year 1 budget as part of the planning process. Some costs like rent and rates, management wages, petrol, packaging etc can be easily broken down to an accurate amount for the month or quarter under review. Other costs like the telephone and electricity bills, vehicle repairs and interest charges may need to be apportioned to give a reasonable monthly or quarterly average.

Fifth, by subtracting the total of the overhead costs of running the business from the gross profit, you arrive at the *net profit* - or loss. If it is a loss the figure on the bottom line will be in brackets.

Doing the 'business sum' on a monthly or quarterly basis is to produce regular *management accounts* which give you the information you need to properly direct the affairs of the enterprise.

The annual accounts

Every enterprise with limited liability, whether it is a cooperative society or a company (see Chapter 7), has to produce properly audited accounts each year. These annual accounts usually consist of three basic documents:

☐ A Profit and Loss Account (sometimes called the revenue account or the income and expenditure account).
☐ The Balance Sheet.
☐ The Statement of Sources and Application of Funds.

The *Profit and Loss Account* shows what profit (or loss) has been made during the financial year. The

Balance Sheet lists what current assets the business has at the end of the financial year (for example, stock in hand, money owed to it and money in the bank) and lists what claims (current liabilities) there are at that time against those assets and which must be paid within one year (for example, money owed for stock, to the Inland Revenue, to repay short-term loans etc). The current liabilities are expected to be covered by the current assets which are therefore usually greater than the liabilities. The Balance Sheet also lists the 'fixed assets' of the business (machinery, plant and equipment etc). The fixed assets are those things expected to last for a reasonable time and each year their value is depreciated, so that over a given period they are written down to a zero value. The total of the fixed and current assets make up the 'gross assets' and after current liabilities have been deducted you are left with the 'net assets' which are represented by the enterprise's capital. If current liabilities exceed current assets then the business is technically insolvent, has lost some of its original capital, and most probably has day-to-day cash problems.

The statement of *Sources and Application of Funds* is a more recent addition to the conventions of annual accounts. This document shows the sources from which funds have come into the business during the year and the uses to which they have been put. It also shows different movements in funds from year to year. In this regard most annual accounts give the previous year's figures for comparison on all three basic accounting documents.

The annual accounts are a statutory requirement and must be filed appropriately with the Registrars of Companies or of Friendly Societies (see Chapter 8). They give a snapshot picture of the business's affairs once a year and are important documents for demonstrating the health of your enterprise to bank managers and others with whom you might be negotiating for funds. How-

		£
Fixed Assets (net of depreciation £1,200)		8,300

Current Assets:	£	£	
Stock	6,000		
Debtors and prepayments	11,000		
Cash at bank and in hand	4,500	21,500	

Less Current Liabilities:			
Creditors and accrued			
expenses	4,750		
Loans	4,000	8,705	

Net current assets		12,750
Net assets		21,050

Represented by:		
Balance brought forward	3,450	
Surplus for the period	5,600	
		9,050
Members loan accounts		4,000
Grants from local authority		8,000
		21,050

(Prepayments are items paid for in the accounting period which cover the period following – typically rent and rates – and accruals are items of expenditure incurred in the period but not yet paid for.)

13. Balance Sheet

ever, the annual accounts are no substitute for your own financial management and control during the year. Once a year is too infrequent to know if your business is healthy and there is usually a considerable time-lag between the end of the financial year, your producing all the information for your accountant, and his coming back with your draft accounts.

Corporation tax

All cooperatives are liable to pay corporation tax on their profits after these have been adjusted to take into account various capital and other allowances. The rate for registered cooperatives has been set at 40 per cent since 1974 and the current small companies rate since the 1983 budget is 38 per cent. The standard current rate of corporation tax is 52 per cent. For most worker and community cooperatives the question of liability to corporation tax in the first years does not arise in the struggle simply to survive and build up. However, it is an area where the services and advice of an accountant are essential to ensure that all the permitted expenditure against surplus is included and that all relevant allowances against tax are claimed.

Other money matters

Income tax: Pay As You Earn (PAYE)
PAYE is a tax collecting system whereby employers deduct income tax from their employees at the point and time of payment and forward the tax to the Inland Revenue. Each employee has a basic tax-free allowance and this is expressed by their tax coding and determined by such factors as whether they are single or married and have other sources of income etc. Tax is payable on all income over the tax-free allowance.

Using the special tables provided by the Inland Revenue the employer deducts the appropriate amount of tax from each employee on a weekly or monthly basis. The amount of tax deducted is notified to each employee by means of the wages slip.

Employers should make monthly payments of collected tax to the Inland Revenue although some elect to do it less frequently. If the tax is not paid over promptly it can all too easily get absorbed into the business's working capital, and when the Inland Revenue demand overdue payments it cannot be readily found. It is good practice either to pay up regularly or to transfer what is due to be paid to a special bank account.

When a new employee starts work he or she should bring with them a P45 form which shows their tax coding, pay to date and tax paid to date. The new employer then deducts tax using these figures and the code number. If a new employee does not have a P45, until he or she obtains a tax coding from the Inland Revenue, the employer has to use the emergency coding which effectively means treating the employee as a single person and paying them each week or month as though it were the first week or month of his/her employment.

A new cooperative enterprise should contact the local tax office in order to obtain an employer's number and the necessary stationery and information for administering the PAYE system. This will include the comprehensive Inland Revenue booklet: *Employer's Guide to PAYE.*

National Insurance and superannuation

Every worker earning more than £32.50 per week (1983 figure) makes a weekly National Insurance payment to the social security system which pays (at least in part) for unemployment benefit, sick pay, maternity benefit, old-age pension etc. All employers also make a payment for each of their employees.

The employee's contribution is deducted, like income tax, on a weekly or monthly basis by the employer and the deduction notified on the wages slip. Special NI tables are available from the Department of Health and Social Security which indicate how much has to be paid both by employer and employee. There are special rates in separate tables for companies with charitable status.

National Insurance contributions are paid over to the Inland Revenue along with income tax. The relevant stationery supplied by the Inland Revenue to send with payments provides for showing how much of each cheque is for income tax and how much for NI. National Insurance payments include a contribution towards the national superannuation scheme which provides for an enhanced pension in old age. However, some enterprises choose to make private arrangements for superannuation and they can contract out of the state scheme.

Value Added Tax (VAT)

VAT is a tax on goods sold, borne by the customer. The standard rate is 15 per cent. Most small businesses registered for VAT are acting as unpaid tax collectors. Whenever they sell anything they must add on VAT and so they collect the tax (this is known as their 'output tax'). Whenever they buy goods and pay for services they are paying VAT (this is known as their 'input tax'). The difference between what they collect and what they pay must be paid over to the Customs and Excise which is the responsible government department. In some cases a business might pay more tax than they collect and consequently they receive a refund.

All businesses with a turnover above £18,000 (1983 figure) must register for VAT. Turnover includes items which are zero rated (ie bear no tax) but excludes items which are exempt (ie outside VAT). Leaflets are available from HM Customs and Excise outlining zero rated and exempt items.

Businesses with a turnover below the minimum figure may be able to register voluntarily at the discretion of the VAT inspectors and it is sometimes worth considering this if your business pays more tax than it collects or if you anticipate your turnover rising quickly. Unless a business is registered for VAT it cannot claim back tax that it pays.

VAT has implications for book-keeping systems in that a record has to be kept of all tax paid and collected. Customs and Excise have devised a number of special schemes to make the work involved easier for different types of business activity and the VAT-man is always prepared to come and discuss whether one of these schemes would be appropriate in a particular case.

Special funding schemes

Cooperatives – especially community cooperatives – which make use of funding schemes such as urban aid and the Manpower Services Commission special programmes will find that each has its

own particular accounting and audit requirements. Each agency will make these known, but
the paperwork involved with MSC schemes
always seems to be considerable.

Bad debts
Bad debts will inevitably happen to your business:
for some reason or other a customer will not be able
to pay. It is important to make provision in your
financial calculations for bad debts in order to
cover yourself against some defaulting. No
business, however, can provide for the failure of a
major customer and this is a common cause of
business closure.

The swifter and more businesslike you are with
your invoicing and your procedure for instantly
chasing up non-payment, the more you will discourage people from trying to delay their payment.
It is the successfully delayed payment which is
given a lower priority and becomes the non-
payment. If customers think they can get away
with it, they are more likely to try it on.

If you do have a persistent bad debt then you can
take legal action through the courts to recover it.
Like all legal action, it costs money and there is no
certainty that the money owed will be recovered.
The full implications of taking legal action need to
be considered and discussed with your solicitors
beforehand. Sometimes the mere threat of action
will make a reluctant payer cough up. It is sensible
sometimes to decide in advance how much you are
willing to spend by way of legal costs and to
instruct your solicitor to incur expenses only up to
a stated ceiling.

Factoring
One means of collecting payments due to you is to
make use of a debt factoring service. The factors
handle all your invoices for you, paying you an
agreed percentage immediately. Once they get
payments in you receive the balance, less the
factor's fee. While debt factoring has some attrac-
tions it is seldom that a small new cooperative

trying to break into a market would be accepted as a client because of its lack of an established track record.

Earning while in receipt of a state benefit

Many people interested in setting up a cooperative are unemployed when they start planning and would like to do some practical testing of the market and start building up their business while in receipt of benefit. However, the law at present does not permit a person to work and continue to claim unemployment and/or supplementary benefit. Nevertheless there are rules governing earnings while on benefit which make it possible to do something, although the financial advantage may be minimal.

If you are in receipt of *unemployment benefit:*

☐ You can earn as much as you like on a Sunday which is outside the scheme, and do not need to declare it. Unemployment benefit is for Monday to Saturday.

☐ In any week you can take one or two days off unemployment benefit and work instead but you must still be available for full-time work. That means your two working days must not stop you going for interviews and accepting a full-time job if one is offered. When you sign on you declare any days' work done and your benefit is then reduced for those days.

☐ You are permitted to earn up to £2 per day (£12 per week if the earnings are spread out over a week) without your benefit being affected. The £2 per day is net earnings after expenses, and expenses can include transport, child-care, advertising, phone calls, equipment or special clothing and even the cost of business premises (if you are self-employed). When you sign on, both earnings and expenses should be declared.

☐ Men with wives who are not working receive a weekly addition for her. The wife can earn up to the amount of the addition (after expenses) and the man will still receive it. If the wife earns more than the addition (after expenses) then the man loses it regardless of by how much his wife's earnings exceed the addition.

If you are in receipt of *supplementary benefit:*

☐ You can earn up to £4 per week (after expenses) before your benefit is reduced and that includes Sundays, as supplementary benefit is for seven days a week.
☐ A man's wife or partner can also earn up to £4 per week (after expenses).
☐ Earnings and expenses should be declared when you sign on.

Although the rules for unemployment benefit give more flexibilty, the reality for many families drawing it is that they have to apply for a 'top-up' from supplementary benefit in order to get enough to live on. Thus the more restrictive supplementary benefit rules apply to them.

If you want to take advantage of the rules permitting these limited earnings it is important that your benefits office knows what you are doing and that you have agreement on what will count as acceptable expenses.

If you are an *old age pensioner:*

☐ Men over 70 and women over 65 can earn as much as they like without their pension being affected (although of course all their income is liable to income tax).
☐ Men between 65 and 70 and women between 60 and 65 can earn up to £57 per week without their pension being affected. For the first £4 earned above £57 the pension is reduced by 5p for every 10p earned. Thereafter it is reduced 5p for each 5p earned.
☐ If a pensioner is claiming a dependant's increase for his wife, the wife can earn up to £45 per week before the dependant's increase is affected. Earnings above £45 affect the increase as described above but only the increase and not the basic pension itself.

If you are on *invalidity benefit* it is sometimes possible to earn up to £20 per week without your benefit being affected, if that work is considered to be 'therapeutic' and either carried out under medical supervision or recommended by your doctor as assisting recovery. It is important that the Insurance Office at the DHSS accepts in advance that working in each particular case has therapeutic value.

Chapter 6
Marketing and Selling

Selling has been described as trying to get the customer to want what the company has, while marketing tries to get the company to produce what the customer wants and needs, thus selling is one particular function in the marketing process. Marketing evolves 'backwards', from the market place to the firm, and is the whole process of identifying consumer needs, organising their production within the constraints of price, place and time, and promoting them to the appropriate customer.

Selling is the specific task at the end of the line. Although for most small cooperatives there is often little distinction between marketing and selling in practice, it is nonetheless important to recognise the need to think through a *marketing strategy* and to avoid the simple assumption that all you have to do is to make your products or provide your service and then go out and sell them. As we shall see, the experience of thinking through a marketing strategy will itself influence the nature and style of the product or service.

Business ideas emerge in a variety of ways as discussed in Chapter 3. A key individual may have a particular skill. Someone comes up with a pet scheme. A brainstorming session throws up a short list of possible ideas. There is an obvious need. More often than not new cooperatives first identify an idea for a service or product which they believe they can provide and set about seeing if there is a market for it. The twin failures of not identifying your market and not being able to sell what you provide are very common in small businesses where the experience and skills of those involved are usually to do with making and doing rather than marketing and selling.

Establishing the existence of a market

Theoretically there are three ways in which you might establish a market and so decide whether you have a potential business:

1. Create the market by stimulating a demand for what you want to make or do.
2. Identify a particular market gap and build your product or service around that.
3. Take your product or service idea and see if there is a market for it, or for an adaptation.

For most cooperatives the starting point is 3, so first analyse in some detail the market information about what the cooperative proposes to do.

Who uses the proposed service/buys the proposed product?
Why do they buy it?
Where do they buy it?
When do they buy it?
How much and how often do they buy it?
Where else can they buy it?

Answers to these questions will build up a picture of the potential market for your scheme. Sources of information and assistance which you might consider in answering these questions are:

Trade magazines in the local library.
Small firms information centre.
Local Enterprise Trusts.
Trade associations.
Local business people (Chambers of Commerce).
Academic institutions seeking project work for students.
People with a sound understanding of the locality.
The Yellow Pages and local newspapers (these

give some idea of the competition).
Just looking and talking around!

Two important questions must always be borne in mind:

□ What is *our* market to be?
□ What is so *special* about us and what we plan to do?

If that sounds like stating the obvious, that is exactly what it is. Marketing is really a question of common sense. *It is a question of trying to make sure, before you commit too much money and effort, that what you are going to do will actually sell.*

What is our market?

The potential market will often prove to be quite large and consist of several distinct parts or segments. For most cooperatives it is important to define quite precisely the particular segment(s) it will aim its output at. Worker and community cooperatives are for the most part small businesses. Their smallness and limited resources are obvious constraints on the type and size of market which they can hope to compete for, let alone satisfy. Geography is another defining constraint on how far the business can reasonably reach out and the distance customers will travel to it.

What is so special about us?
Your business needs to be able to claim some particular advantage for its services or products over any competitors, and this advantage is something which should be quickly and readily recognisable by potential customers. It may be that what you are doing is unique, but more usually it will be that you have found an 'edge' over your competitors. Is it that your product or service is better? Or is it cheaper? Is it where you are based? Is it your 'service with a smile'? Is it the after-sales service? In the case of cooperatives, the

close links with a particular local community can themselves give an advantage.

Having identified your target market and carefully thought through what advantages your particular proposals have, you are in a position to plan your *marketing strategy*. This entails taking decisions on a number of practical factors sometimes referred to as the four Ps: product, price, promotion and place.

Product/Service

Decide exactly what you are going to do:

Quality.
Details of design, colour, finish etc.
What your service will include (and what you will *not* offer to do).
Packaging.
Guarantees, after-sales service, return of faulty goods etc

Remember when making all these decisions to check that you can do what you intend, that you can obtain what you need to do it and that it does not significantly change the costs already estimated in your business plan.

Price

As part of your business plan you will have calculated at least a basic minimum price per unit to ensure that the business breaks even. That price will have been based on 'cost plus': that is the cost of producing the goods or service, plus a proportion for business running costs (overheads or fixed costs), plus a margin added on for profit. As part of your marketing strategy you need to consider two other approaches as part of the process of fixing a price.

☐ *What the customer will pay*. It may be that you can make a much greater profit, have different price bands for different categories of customer, or that you have an up-market range and a down-market range.

□ *What the competition is doing.* What is the 'going rate' for what you are planning? What are competitors charging?

If what the customers will pay and the going rate are both less than your cost-plus price it means going back to rethink either your idea or your target market or to reassess your expected costs.

A further dimension often included in cooperative pricing is that of providing good value for money. Most cooperatives' objectives include the intention to benefit the local community. That benefit might take the form of keeping prices low in a particular locality or for a particular group of customers.

Promotion

Products or services need the assistance of well devised schemes of promotion, although this does not necessarily mean that the business must incur heavy advertising costs. The local press may provide editorial news coverage about a community cooperative or a local workers' initiative and that amounts to free advertising. Local radio and television may also help. Other methods of promotion include attendance at trade exhibitions, sending out mail shots and preparing promotional leaflets for general distribution. Sales promotion techniques associated with the point of sale include special offers, price reductions and special packaging and displays.

Place

Place means not only where the selling will be done but also the method of distribution. Is the product or service to be sold direct through shops or wholesale distributors; will there be direct sales from the factory or by mail order; will agents be appointed? What types of outlet will the business concentrate on and what does that mean in terms of distribution costs and transport? What does it mean in terms of stock levels needed at each outlet point and how frequently do outlets require visiting?

As you work through the practical questions of product, price, promotion and place the choices you make add up to your marketing strategy. All the choices are variables which must be adjusted from time to time in the light of experience and of developments as your business theory becomes reality. The strategy must be under constant review.

Business growth and development

In order to survive a business must adapt to external changes. In order to expand it must be receptive to new ideas. Few products or services remain the same for ever. Technological innovation, fashions of taste and style, invention all contribute to a business environment in which the pace of change is nowadays quite phenomenal. There is a need to look and plan ahead. Planning can focus in any of four areas:

- ☐ Look for ways of expanding your existing market.
- ☐ Consider whether you can compete in a wider market by making some adaptations to your product/service and to the variables in your marketing strategy.
- ☐ Consider whether you can develop your product or service so as to improve, extend or replace it.
- ☐ Consider whether your business can diversify: go into something different which means a new idea and a new market, a new business plan and a new marketing strategy.

Selling

Selling is a vitally important function of marketing. In the small cooperative, marketing and selling go hand in hand and it can often be hard to distinguish the two except theoretically.

Selling is a rare skill: not everybody has the confidence, style or ability to go out and sell.

If your cooperative can find one or two members who positively like selling that is a great advantage. It is also important to respect the feelings of people who do not want to sell. Many people can think of nothing more daunting and a reluctant sales person will not be a good one.

Although it is desirable to have a recognised sales person or people, the reality for many small cooperatives is that almost everybody gets involved in selling at some time or other. For 'amateur' sales people some common-sense (but often overlooked) points are worth bearing in mind.

1. *Presentation.* It is important that the goods or services are well presented. Packaging should be pleasing and 'smart'. Services should be offered in a professional way which gives an immediate impression that the company offering the service knows exactly what it is doing.
2. *Reliability.* The cooperative must be able to fulfil its promises. Time schedules must be kept: there is nothing more frustrating for a customer than to be kept waiting while deadlines come and go without result.
3. *Promptness.* Promptness is likely to ensure repeat orders. Enquiries handled with alacrity and prompt deliveries always give a good impression (so does prompt invoicing!).
4. *Punctuality.* Nothing can be more irritating than sales personnel (or others) arriving late for appointments. In the hustle of winning business such things can be crucial in selling (or not selling) goods and services.
5. *Personal appearance.* From the customer's viewpoint, the initial impressions of the cooperative may well be formed by the personal appearance of the individual doing the selling. It is, therefore, important for this person to look

97

neat, tidy and smart. This is not to say that smart-looking people do not sell poor quality goods or services: simply that signs of scruffiness may inhibit potential customers from further investigation. Image and first impressions are important.
6. *Telephone manner.* A telephone call is often the first contact between a business and its customer. A pleasant telephone manner, quickly and accurately answered enquiries, all help create the right image for the company.

Export

If you are considering export enquire first at your nearest Small Firms Information Centre and read the free Department of Industry booklet *How to start exporting.* Contact the British Overseas Trade Board for the free pamphlet outlining their services.

Chapter 7

Legal Structures

Anybody can set up in business, either on their own or in association with others. In the first instance you are a *sole trader*, in the second you are in *partnership*. If you trade under a name different from your real name(s) then you must display the real names and addresses of the owners/partners publicly at your premises and on your business stationery. There is no legal process to becoming a sole trader or a partnership – you simply start trading. However, with partnerships it is usually advisable for the partners to have a legal agreement to define the ground rules for their working association.

Partnerships

A partnership could be a group of people working together cooperatively and thus in practice a workers' cooperative. Equally (and more usually) it could be a small group of people who employ others and share the profits created by the business among themselves. While a partnership can be run as a cooperative, there are neither safeguards that it will continue as such nor a clear framework of cooperative structure or rules. The crunch question is often expressed as whether in a partnership of ten professional people the typist and the tea-person become the eleventh and twelfth equal partners or whether they become mere employees.

Sole traders and partnerships do not have limited liability: if the business gets into trouble the owner or the partners are entirely responsible for all liabilities and their own personal possessions can be called in to meet them. All partners are responsible for the business decisions of each partner and also for the consequences. In other words, there is no distinction at law between the business affairs and the private affairs of those concerned.

Cooperative incorporation

Worker and community cooperatives will adopt a proper legal structure for their business by becoming incorporated either as a cooperative society or as a limited company. The legal structure:

☐ Gives limited liability.
☐ Defines the objectives and the purpose of the enterprise.
☐ Defines who the membership will be, and who the Directors/Committee of Management.
☐ Sets out the rules of operation.
☐ States what will happen to the profits.
☐ States what will happen to any assets if the enterprise has to be wound up.

Cooperatives and companies

Cooperative societies are registered under the Industrial and Provident Societies Acts 1965-78. Cooperative law is administered by the Registrar of Friendly Societies. The constitution of a cooperative society is called the rules. Members of cooperative societies have shares in their society but these shares are often no more than a one person-one share membership ticket. The nominal share is the extent of the members' financial liability for outstanding debts in the event of a liquidation. There must be a minimum of seven founder members.

Companies are incorporated under the Companies Acts 1948-81. Company law is administered by the Registrar of Companies. The constitution of a company is called the memorandum and articles of association. Two people are the minimum required to form a company.

The most common type of company is a private company limited by shares. The shareholders are the owners of the company. Their shares represent the money which they have put into it and which they will lose should the company founder. Profits not put back into the company are distributed according to shareholdings.

Attempts have been made to write the constitution of share companies in such a way as to accord with cooperative principles and practice, but it is more usual for cooperatives to use the form of a *company limited by guarantee.* Guarantee companies have members rather than shareholders and their personal liability for debts in the event of liquidation is restricted to a (usually) nominal amount (often just £1).

There are now a number of model constitutions (see pages 116-23) using both cooperative and company law and suitable variously for worker and community cooperatives. Most newly formed cooperative groups can now either adopt one of the existing models as it is or can make some slight adaptations to suit their particular locality and circumstances.

Limited liability

Limited liability means that the trading organisation, *not* the individual members, is responsible for all debts, liabilities and legal obligations. In effect, the business has its own legal existence separate from its members and members' personal assets cannot be called in to meet the debts of the business apart, that is, from their nominal guarantee or their shareholding. The distinct legal personality of the cooperative or company establishes its separateness and thus its limited liability. Limited liability does not absolve the Directors or Committee of Management of a cooperative from acting responsibly with regard to business practice. They may not continue to trade if the business is known to be insolvent unless they have come to some arrangement with the main creditors. Continuing to trade when insolvent and without an arrangement can render the limited liability of the business null and void.

Objectives

It is important to be clear about what your cooperative aims to achieve and the things it proposes to do to achieve those aims.

Most community cooperatives aim to create jobs for local people, often for the unemployed in particular. Some aim also to provide locally needed services, others to provide training opportunities. Others again wish to focus their attention on the young; some see themselves as a focus for various types of both community and economic development and so aim to act more as neighbourhood development agencies.

The decisions about what you want to do will find expression in the constitution of your cooperative, but almost more important is the process of discussing what you want to do and arriving at an agreement. That process will help concentrate and strengthen the cooperative determination of the founders.

Most community cooperatives intend to be multi-functional and engage in a wide range of both trading and other activity in order to achieve the desired aims. In practice, of course, many end up concentrating on one particular activity, but it is important to include in the constitution everything you might want to do in the future rather than find yourselves either restricted or having to make constitutional amendments. A cooperative or company can only do what is specifically authorised by its constitution.

Community cooperative or company

Key objects of model constitution

1. The relief of poverty by the alleviation of unemployment for the residents of . . .

2. To provide and assist in the provision of training opportunities . . . with a view to teaching particular skills which will assist (local) people in finding work.

3. To carry on business in manufacturing, construction, recycling and service industries with a view to furthering the objects above mentioned.

(Local Enterprise Advisory Project memorandum and articles for community business.)

A workers' cooperative is more likely to be monofunctional with its main business activity as its primary and most emphasised objective. However, it is important to ensure that the cooperative's constitution gives it the authority to do all that it may require. It is equally important that intending

---

Worker cooperatives

Key objects of model rules

2. The objects of the cooperative shall be to carry on the business as a bona fide cooperative society of

   (a) Manufacturing or selling . . .
   Providing the service of . . .
   (b) Manufacturing or selling or hiring whether as wholesalers, retailers, agents, or otherwise, such other goods (or providing such service) as may be determined by a General Meeting.

   In carrying out the aforesaid objects the cooperative shall have regard to promoting the physical, mental and spiritual well-being of the community and especially those who participate in the activities of the cooperative by reason of employment in or purchasing from or selling to the cooperative and to assist people in need by any means whatsoever.

3. Powers. The cooperative shall have power to do all things necessary or expedient for the fulfilment of its objects, . . .

(Industrial Common Ownership Movement Model Rules 1977)

---

worker cooperators discuss not only their internal aims and procedures but also how they wish to relate to the wider community and whether they have any broader objectives beyond running a successful business to give them a reasonable living. Failure to have some agreement on the question of wider objectives at an early stage can lead to disagreement later.

Membership

A fundamental cooperative principle is that of *open membership*. The constitution defines who can be a member and then all those who meet that definition can of right be members of the cooperative.

In the case of worker cooperatives the right to membership is usually restricted to persons working – full- or part-time – in the business. It is quite usual for a cooperative to establish a probationary period for new members and so give a chance for existing members and the prospective new member to get to know each other and find out if they suit. A workers' cooperative is a rather special organisation and each will have its own ways of working and its own aims. It can well happen that a prospective member will find him/herself uncomfortable in the cooperative situation or unable to adapt to the cooperative demands.

Once a new worker has completed any probationary period he/she has a right to membership which cannot be refused. In some situations eligible workers do not take up that entitlement and remain employees. The Industrial Common Ownership Act 1976 specifically states (para 2(2)(b)) that at least a majority of workers should be members if the enterprise is to be a bona fide workers' cooperative.

Community cooperatives are usually based on a geographical locality and any person living there is entitled to become a member. In many community cooperatives people who work in the defined area – which is also the area of benefit – are also entitled to membership. In some cases, especially in housing estates, the community cooperative arises out of an existing community or tenants' association and that association which itself has open membership nominates the members of the community cooperative or company.

The final decision on applicants for membership of a community cooperative usually rests with the board of directors at any time although the original founding members will probably have established guidelines about what, if any, grounds there might be for refusal. A problem more familiar to community cooperatives, especially in urban areas, is how to encourage more people to join and so contribute to local economic development.

Most community cooperatives recognise the need to involve people from outside to bring in skills and expertise which may not be locally available. Some allow a limited number of 'outsider' members, others make arrangements for co-opting extra directors or for non-voting advisers to attend board or other important meetings.

The founder members of any cooperative are those who are in at the start and sign the cooperative society's rules or the guarantee company's memorandum and articles of association (depending on how it is set up). It is usual for the founder members to act as the first committee of management or board of directors.

The members of a cooperative own it and control its affairs on a one person–one vote basis. Control and management may be vested in a committee of management or board of directors and in turn the managers and others, but the ultimate accountability, and therefore the ultimate control, rests with the members of the cooperative in a general meeting.

For community cooperatives it can be somewhat tricky agreeing a definition of the geographical area of benefit. A balance has to be struck between having an area with some sense of identity or community, a large enough area on which to base economic initiatives, and an area which can conveniently be described. For this latter purpose local authority electoral wards are often used.

Rules of operation

It is important for any organisation to have clear rules because they set the framework within which the members of the company operate and establish the democratic process for settling disputes. For a company the operating procedures are set out in the *articles of association* (the objects having been set down in the memorandum). For a cooperative society both objects and procedures are included in the *rules*. Much of the detail of how a company or cooperative should operate is prescribed by law but the founding members have to make important choices on a number of matters. The articles or rules set down:

- [ ] How people become members and cease to be members.
- [ ] The size of the board of directors/management committee, its method of election and how long one person can remain on it.
- [ ] The powers of the board/committee and how the meetings should be run.
- [ ] Whether the chairperson has a casting vote.
- [ ] Voting procedures both for board/committee and general meetings.
- [ ] The size of a quorum for board/committee and general meetings. (A quorum is the smallest number of people who *must* be present if the meeting is to proceed and any business be legally transacted.)
- [ ] The calling of general meetings, how much notice must be given and who is entitled to receive papers.
- [ ] The size of the membership subscription (if any).
- [ ] The powers which can be given to subcommittees and who might be on them.

☐ How far the accounts may be open to inspection of the membership and/or the public.

☐ The statutory requirements about keeping minutes of meetings, proper books of account, holding an AGM and audit.

In addition to the formal rules set down in the articles of association or cooperative rules, it is quite usual for a cooperative to establish its own *house rules* through decisions taken by a general meeting of the membership or by the board of directors/committee of management. These regulations assist in day-to-day operation and establish policies particular to the enterprise. House rules might cover such things as contributions to a social fund, disciplinary and grievance procedures, recruitment policy, wage ratios: in short any decision which the cooperative decides to implement as a general rule for organising itself and its affairs provided that this in no way contradicts the legal constitution.

Capital

One fundamental principle of a cooperative is the fact that the members both own and control the enterprise. In workers' cooperatives this is usually expressed by the phrase *labour hires capital*, rather than labour being hired by capital. For the community cooperative it means that local residents own and control the enterprise and they therefore determine its policies and development rather than outside entrepreneurs and investors.

Cooperative constitutions preclude any external capital holdings because to admit external capital as equity would be to admit an element of external control. Most founders of cooperatives do not have significant funds to invest in their enterprises, although some worker cooperative founders are able to contribute to the start-up capital from redundancy payments or other savings and some community cooperatives (notably in the Highlands and Islands of Scotland) have raised significant sums of start-up capital, and they and others have also obtained grant-aid from public authorities. A guarantee company structure has no mechanism to provide for shareholding by members whereas a cooperative society does (see below). In general though, cooperatives are financed not by equity, but by loans and this can be a significant weakness. The cooperative movement is actively discussing the establishment of a cooperative equity finance company which could invest in cooperatives without prejudicing the fundamental principles of worker or community control.

A further dilemma regarding the capitalisation of cooperatives concerns how far the assets of a cooperative should be collectively owned (held in common) or whether individual members can claim ownership of a portion of the assets. Opinions are divided and hotly contested and the existing model rules (see pages 116-23) allow a variety of formulae. The community business model constitution developed through the Local Enterprise Advisory Project in Scotland and the Industrial Common Ownership Movement's worker cooperative constitutions are based firmly on collective ownership. However, Highlands and Islands Community Cooperatives permit individual shareholdings, although as cooperative shares they bring a limited dividend and voting remains one member–one vote rather than one share–one vote, while the constitution being developed by Job Ownership Ltd and partly based on the Mondragon experience (see page 16) sets out to enable cooperative members to have personal ownership over part of the enterprise but also to take a capital asset away when they leave.

The balance between collective ownership and a sense, if not reality, of individual ownership is one which each cooperative must discuss and decide for itself. The idea of mutuality which is at the heart of cooperation suggests collective ownership and equal sharing. However, the cooperative which is in part financed by members' contributions will find it easier to raise other loans. It is true also that many cooperatives have had to wrestle with the problem of how to reward the founder members for their hard work and low wages to start the enterprise up, especially if a founder member leaves just when the business has become established and can start to pay its workers well. The longer people work in a cooperative the more they begin to look at what they might expect on retirement from the business of which they are part owner.

Profit

There are three ways in which a workers' cooperative might use its profits:

☐ Reinvestment in the business
☐ Distribution to members
☐ Development of a project for local social or community benefit.

Some cooperatives prescribe in their rules a minimum or maximum percentage for one, two or all of these categories, others will leave the decision to the wishes of the members on an annual basis.

It is usual for a community company to prohibit distribution of profits to individual members and to ensure that any profits are used to build up the enterprise and create more jobs or put into some local scheme of community benefit.

Dissolution

Winding up a cooperative is a long way from the founders' minds when they are struggling to set it up, but it is important to be clear about disposal of the remaining assets at such a time, and this is spelled out in the constitution. Most common is the dissolution clause which prohibits distribution to individual members and insists on any assets being transferred to another organisation with similar objectives. A cooperative which believes more in individual ownership and personal member benefit would adopt a dissolution clause permitting distribution of all or some remaining assets to members. If nothing is specified about the distribution of remaining assets then they will automatically go to the members at the time of dissolution.

Philosophy

Cooperatives are about ideals as well as running businesses. Although the legal structure lays down the objectives, it mainly covers rules of organisation and procedure and does not really express a philosophy. Sometimes it is helpful to write down the ideals and values which lie at the foundation of the cooperative and which should have been thrashed out in early discussions when deciding objectives, membership, distribution of profits and so forth. A *preamble* of this nature to the constitution does not have the force of law but it does let outsiders know what the company stands for and it gives a clear statement for prospective members to agree or disagree with before joining.

Preambles to constitutions

Scott Bader Commonwealth

WE, the Subscribers of the Memorandum of Association of THE SCOTT BADER COMMONWEALTH LIMITED, hereby express—

The Commonwealth is a duly registered Company limited by guarantee, without share capital, and has been founded on the belief that a socially responsible undertaking cannot exist merely in its own interests. It is part of the whole national and international community, and as such it has responsibilities which extend far beyond its factory walls;

Our purpose in making our stand is for a better, peaceful Industrial and Social Order, for which purpose we believe that we must obey the simple laws of Christianity in our daily lives, and present an alternative to a war-based capitalist economy on the one hand and to Communism on the other. Thus we strive to follow a business policy which calls for a fundamental reconstruction as indicated by the following seven paragraphs:

1. Since in our time the seeds of war go deeper into the life of the nations than ever before, and since not only the power politics of Government, but also the profit-seeking of Capitalists and the pressure for higher wages on the part of the Employed, are amongst the causes of war, we all need to walk humbly and to ponder over the problem of conducting our individual and corporate life in accordance with the demands of peace against the current of a society war-based between Capitalism and Communism.

2. We appeal to everyone, and particularly to our fellow business men, to ask themselves to what extent violence resides in the demands we make upon the earth's resources and the available raw materials by reason of our self-indulgent existence, and what is to be our personal contribution to the realisation of peace.

3. In view of these considerations we feel convinced that far-reaching reconstruction cannot be delayed and that the principle of Common-ownership in industry, based on the requirements of a peaceful society, represent essential steps towards a true Christian Industrial and Social Order.

4. By establishing Common-ownership in industry we mean such a fundamental reconstruction so that under-takings are communally owned and cooperatively run, and show that team-work which is neither Collectivism nor Individualism, depending on leadership founded on approval rather than dictation within a framework of freedom of conscience and obedience to God. This involves a self-divestment of privilege and power on the part of the present employers and shareholders, and on the part of the employees the acceptance of their full share of responsibility for the policy, efficiency and general welfare of the undertaking.

5. In accordance with the well-known testimony of the Quakers and other Christian Pacifist movements against war, we reaffirm that among the requirements of a peaceful society is included a reconstruction without participation in industrial strife and international war; and a refusal to take an active part in rearmament.

6. Whilst we do not admit that because we pay taxes, and supply goods which ultimately may have an application in war, or make other indirect contri-butions which the State is partly using for military purposes, we are thereby compromised and committed to bend our knees to the military machine, we realise the dilemma involved in our attempt to conduct business on lines not approved by the Government nor the large majority of our fellow men. We recall that social progress has always had its roots in the activities of a small minority retaining faith in face of overwhelming opposition.

7. Furthermore, we believe that to live and to order our affairs in that spirit which takes away the occasion for war, and the acceptance and fulfilment of the above principles, will call forth that individual discipline which is a first essential for the bringing in of a new society.

28 April 1951

Flagstone Enterprises Limited

Ferguslie Park is recognised as the most deprived area in Renfrew District. There are many indicators used to measure deprivation and one that is fundamental is the level of male unemployment. In Ferguslie Park, for instance, male unemployment has been in excess of 25 per cent of the working male population for some three years.

This level of unemployment is totally unacceptable and as long as it exists, the chances of any other community initiatives having any real impact in Ferguslie Park are minimal. Much has been written about the causes of unemployment, but in Ferguslie Park it is the effects that are most striking – nearly 50 per cent of all households have someone dependent on supplementary benefit. The real poverty exists in terms of the number of fuel supply disconnections, rent arrears and lack of basic household goods, like washing machines. There is also general depression in an area where so many are unemployed and one hears daily of either hospital admissions for depression or criminal activity caused by sheer frustration. The stigma of a Ferguslie address can adversely influence chances of re-employment.

With this background, Ferguslie League of Action Groups recognise that the creation of employment is necessary if any of FLAG's other initiatives are to have a chance of success. But the creation of employment in this respect is seen as complementing the other work that FLAG does: ie, it has to be on behalf of the community, or at least any money or goods coming from the creation of employment must be used on behalf of the community.

This is a basic recognition of the fact that too often in the past the people of Ferguslie Park have been exploited for profit and then discarded when it has suited the employer. In recent years many hundreds have been thrown out of work as local factories making bricks, toilets, threads, carpets, jam and bedding have closed down and moved their operations elsewhere leaving Ferguslie people without a livelihood. FLAG

---

does not want to overthrow the world market system but feels that any employment created should be on behalf of the local community and in its control. The community's needs and not those of world markets will decide the future of this company.

FLAG's proposal simply is to create a 'community company' where all control and all profits are in the hands of the local community, to be used for the improvement of the local community.

Details of how this will be done are contained in the constitution which follows.

(Abridged) *July 1979*

Model constitutions

A number of model constitutions have been devised and tested, and cooperative society rules approved as model rules by the Registrar of Friendly Societies. The main models available which have been tried and tested, are:

Worker Cooperatives
☐ Industrial Common Ownership Movement model rules (ICOM 1982) for a workers' cooperative society.
☐ ICOM model memorandum and articles of association (ICOM 1982) for a common ownership company (the Scottish Cooperatives Development Committee uses its own model memorandum and articles of association for a cooperative company which are largely similar to the ICOM model memorandum and articles).
☐ Cooperative Development Agency model rules (CDA 1982) for a workers' cooperative society.

Community Cooperatives
☐ Local Enterprise Advisory Project model memorandum and articles of association for a community company.
☐ Highlands and Islands Development Board model rules for a community cooperative society.

□ Cooperative Development Agency model rules (CDA 1980) for a neighbourhood services cooperative.

Other

□ Cooperative Union general rules for an industrial and provident cooperative society.

In the table below these alternative model rules are compared.[1] In addition to the models listed *Job Ownership Ltd* (see page 157) has reached an advanced stage of preparing a model memorandum and articles of association which allow for the assets of the enterprise to be held partly in common and partly by individual members' shareholdings. Individual shareholdings consist of an initial stake paid by a member on joining (or over the first months of working) and an allocation to his/her share account of a share in distributed profits. (In the same way share accounts will bear a proportion of an annual loss.) On retirement or leaving, the member will be able to sell his share to the company and so benefit from an accumulated sum (assuming the company to have been profitable).

The Industrial Common Ownership Movement Ltd (see page 156) is preparing a cooperative partnership agreement to permit the setting up of a partnership which meets the basic cooperative principles.

The Cooperative Development Agency is preparing notes about the possible formation of *Employee Participation Cooperatives* which could be the means of the workers in a conventional operating company holding shares collectively in their enterprise. While this would give them ony part ownership it is suggested that this structure might attract outside capital into the enterprise in a way which is not possible in a true cooperative.

---

1. The basis for this table first appeared in *Whose Business is Business?* 1981, the report of the Community Business Ventures Unit published by the Calouste Gulbenkian Foundation.

Further, the EPC might acquire full ownership of the enterprise in the future by buying back the shares held by other investors.

Instant Muscle, (see page 157), which is a national network of young persons' cooperatives, has produced model rules which suitably adapt the existing models. These provide for working members, corporate members and 'other persons who reside in the area in which the cooperative sells its services and who may from time to time give help or advice to the cooperative', stipulate the appointment of a controller to manage day-to-day affairs and permit the appointment of up to three advisers. Assets are distributed on dissolution as decided by a general meeting.

Beechwood College, (see page 157), has recently published a draft model memorandum and articles of association for a community cooperative. Membership includes employees, volunteer workers and representatives from the local community. A particular feature is the inclusion of a requirement to have an annual social audit carried out by an independent assessor. A detailed procedure is spelt out which has the intention of making the social audit as important and binding to the cooperative as its annual financial audit. There is also the suggestion for establishing (and a draft constitution for) a social council to be responsible for determining the social policy of the cooperative and for ensuring that the social accounts are properly carried out each year.

The *Cooperative Development Agency* is discussing a set of model rules for a community cooperative and a draft is available although it was not yet registered as a model in August 1983.

Model constitutions for worker and community cooperatives

Model	Objects	Membership
ICOM MODEL RULES (ICOM 1982) Workers' cooperative (Industrial and Provident Society – – I & PS)	Covers manufacturing and/or selling and/or providing services. Also states that the society has social objectives in addition to commercial ones. It is concerned with the 'physical', 'mental' and 'spiritual' well-being of its members and the wider community.	The basic common ownership principle is that the enterprise is controlled and owned by the people working in it. Anyone working in the coop whether full or part time or voluntary is eligible for membership if they are over 18. Each member may hold only one share without dividend (a non-transferable membership ticket). Each coop must decide whether it wants contributions from members in loans.
ICOM MEMORANDUM AND ARTICLES OF ASSOCIATION Company limited by guarantee and without share capital Workers' cooperative (company)	In addition to the wide commerical objectives of the company, there is a clause stating a commitment to support the concept of common ownership in industry and commerce and to support the Industrial Common Ownership Movement. In carrying out its objectives the company will consider the 'physical, mental and spiritual' well-being of those who are employed in the company or others generally in need.	Only employees of the company may be members. No member has more than one vote. Members may contribute via loan stock. The maximum liability is £1.

Management	Profits	Notes
The coop must have a committee of not less than five or more than 19 (with these numbers committees and the general meeting can be the same). Above 20 a representative structure is recommended. Only members may vote, but it is possible to invite non-members to join in an advisory capacity. The committee is also responsible for the appointment of managers. Ultimate control lies with the members in the general meeting and committees and managers are given discretionary powers to do a job.	The general meeting will decide the proportional split between the following three areas to which profits must be applied: 1. A reserve for the continuation and development of the coop. 2. A bonus to members. 3. Payment to social and charitable objectives.	1. Membership is only open to workers except for non-working members – who may resign later and then cannot be replaced. (A Coop Society must have at least seven members.) 2. On dissolution, remaining assets must go to other common ownerships or to charitable purposes.
A general council between three and 20 people will be elected at the AGM. Only members of the company may be elected to the council. Outsiders may be invited to attend general meetings. The general council is the main management body of the company. It may delegate its powers to any sub-committee.	The income and property of the company are solely for the promotion of its objectives. No portion is to be paid to the members except wages, bonuses and expenses incurred for the company. The general meeting shall decide the proportion for the allocation of profit in the following three ways: 1. A general reserve for the continuation and development of the company. 2. A bonus to members. 3. Payments to social and charitable objects and to support ICOM.	1. A company needs only two members to register. 2. In the event of dissolution, after debts/liabilities are satisfied, any balance of assets must be transferred to other common ownerships with compatible objectives or to charitable purposes.

Model	Objects	Membership
CDA MODEL RULES (CDA 1982) Workers' cooperative (I & PS)	Covers manufacturing and/or selling and/or providing services.	Membership open to founders, employees and others – society, company, corporate body or individual – approved by the committee of management. Only members may hold shares up to the legal maximum.

LOCAL ENTERPRISE ADVISORY PROJECT COMMUNITY BUSINESS MEMORANDUM AND ARTICLES OF ASSOCIATION
 	
Company limited by guarantee without share capital
 	
A multi-functional community company
	1. The relief of poverty by the alleviation of un-employment principally for the residents of . . .
	2. To provide or assist the provision of training opportunities for residents.
	3. To carry on business in manufacturing/construction, recycling and service industries, to further the above objects.
	4. To borrow and raise money for the purpose of the company.
	5. To print/publish any newspapers, periodicals, books or leaflets necessary for the promotion of its objects.
	6. To take any necessary steps to secure funds for the company.
		Anyone resident/working in . . . is eligible. Non-residents/workers can be nominated by two members – this category must not exceed 50 per cent of total membership.
		    No employee may become a member.
		    All members will pay an annual subscription, the amount to be decided by the board of directors, but will not exceed £10 unless the consent of a general meeting is obtained.
		    Members have only one vote. The convenor of any meeting shall not have a second/casting vote.

Management	Profits	Notes
A committee of between five and seven members to be elected by and from members. A manager can be appointed by the committee.	Profits will be applied as decided by a general meeting in the following ways: 1. General reserve. 2. Bonus to workers. 3. Interest on shares (up to a rate of 5 per cent). 4. Social and charitable purposes. A bonus of £1 shares can be issued to members in proportion to an increase in value of the assets.	On dissolution, assets can be distributed as members wish.
There will be a minimum of four and a maximum of 20 member directors and four co-opted directors. Co-opted directors cannot be employees. The entire business of the company shall be managed by the board except for any activities that can only be exercised by the company in a general meeting. The board has the power to appoint and remove paid employees. Employees are to nominate representatives to the board. They can only speak/advise and have no vote.	There can be no distribution of profits among members of the company and on dissolution remaining assets must be given or transferred to another charitable organisation with similar objectives. The income and property of the company shall be applied only to the promotion of the objects of the company (that is to develop the business, create jobs and be used for community benefit) and there will be no dividend or bonus to the members of the company.	This model has been accepted in in Scotland in most cases for charitable status.

Running Your Own Cooperative

Model	Objects	Membership
COMMUNITY CO-OPERATIVES HIDB MODEL RULES (I & PS)	The objects are to carry on virtually any activity designated to be for the benefit of the members.	Membership is open to those over 18 who now or did reside in the community served by the coop, and the HIDB and any other corporate body if decided by a general meeting. Members must have at least one share the value of which is set by each coop and may be paid in instalments if the coop chooses. Each member has one vote.

Management	Profits	Notes
Each coop will have a management committee of between five and 15 members. The members of the first committee shall be the subscribers of the application for registration. Subsequent committees to be elected at AGMs. The committee exercises all powers not required to be exercised in an AGM. Only members of the coop may be on the committee.	Profits are to be applied: 1. To a general reserve for the continuation and development of the coop. 2. Paying interest on paid-up share capital. 3. Paying a bonus to members in proportion to the business transactions by them with the coop at rates and terms dictated by the general meeting. 4. Social and charitable objects. The proportion and manner of the distribution of profits shall be decided by the general meeting.	1. There is a clear reference to 'community' in the membership rule. 2. Corporate bodies, such as local authorities or companies, can be members. 3. The HIDB is unlikely to act as a sponsoring body for schemes outside its area. However, the potential exists for re-registering the model or even copying it and deleting any reference to the HIDB.

Running Your Own Cooperative

Model	Objects	Membership
NEIGHBOUR-HOOD CO-OPERATIVES CDA MODEL RULES (CDA 1980) (I & PS)	The rules refer to trades, industries or businesses to be carried on for the benefit of members – or any services which members deem necessary. 　There is no specific reference to social objectives, except that the objects must be for the benefit of members – therefore, presumably social objectives could be included; or the services described could be of community benefit.	Membership is for full- and part-time employees and others who reside in the neighbourhood and give occasional help. 　Members must be over 16. Shares are limited to one per member and have a nominal value of £1. Coops may make loans from potential members a condition of membership.
CO-OPERATIVE UNION General rules for an I & PS	Retail, service, provision, manufacturer, producer, grower of any goods. 　Societies using these model rules must become members of the Cooperative Union.	Membership is open to anyone over 16, holding at least one £1 share. Societies may take shares. No individual member may have more than £1,000 shares. Each society may stipulate a minimum number of shares required for membership. In addition an application fee can be designated. The total value of the shares taken does not need to be paid fully at once. All members have one vote regardless of the number of shares held.

Management	Profits	Notes
There will be a committee of between three and nine members elected at the AGM. Only members may be elected. The committee may exercise all such powers as may be exercised by the society.	Profits are to be applied: 1. To a reserve for the continuation of the society. 2. To a bonus for full- and part-time employees. 3. To the establishment of other neighbourhood coops or 4. To a charity. The proportions to be detailed by the General Meeting.	1. There may be a problem over the definition of a 'neighbourhood' – how wide an area this can cover. It prevents use by 'communities of interest' as opposed to 'communities of a geographical area'. 2. Membership is not just for paid workers but for others from the community who wish to help.
The annual meeting shall appoint the directors and fix their remuneration. The meeting shall have a chairman who does not vote unless a casting vote is necessary. A director must be a member of the society. The manager and secretary of the society are responsible to the directors. Special rules must be made to allow employees to become directors. However, no more than two employees may serve on the board at any one time.	The profits are to be applied as follows: 1. Payment of interest on share capital. 2. A reserve fund for the society. 3. A sum for the promotion of education, culture or recreation. 4. Subscriptions to the funds of the Coop Party. 5. A dividend on the value of purchases from the society to members and if desired non-members.	1. Membership not defined. 2. Rules developed for coop retail societies: hence the dividend to consumers. 3. Subscription to Coop Party might deter some potential users.

Charitable status

The definition of a charity was first set down by law in the sixteenth century, and to a large extent does not correspond with popular thinking about what could reasonably be considered charitable today. A company which is trading commercially and making profits as a significant activity cannot be a charity. However, many community companies can be considered charities if their main work is to do with training, giving information and advice, developing business ideas and sponsoring other projects. To qualify for charitable status a company:

☐ Must not distribute profits to members.
☐ May not have employees as directors.
☐ Must pledge any assets remaining on dissolution to another (similar) charity.
☐ Will mention the relief of poverty and/or education and training as part of its objectives.

Once any particular trading activity becomes viable and profitable, the company will float it off as a separate non-charitable trading company which in turn might pledge its profits to the charitable 'parent' company. In some cases, community companies which successfully develop a particular business enterprise encourage it to set up as an autonomous workers' cooperative.

In Scotland, where there are no Charity Commissioners, the model memorandum and articles of association developed by the Local Enterprise Advisory Project have generally been accepted for charitable status by the Inland Revenue. A community company with charitable status may not have worker directors although non-voting employee representatives may attend and speak at board meetings and receive all relevant papers.

The main financial advantage of charitable status is relief from the National Insurance surcharge. Additionally, some charitable trusts can give grants only to registered charities although for the most part it is the charitable objectives which are important rather than the registered status.

Constitutional changes

Any changes to the rules of a cooperative society have to be approved by the Registrar of Friendly Societies and officially registered by him. A company's memorandum and articles of association can be changed by a general meeting agreeing to it by the necessary three-quarters majority and that change being notified to the Registrar of Companies.

Audit and annual returns

Each year all cooperative societies and companies must have their accounts audited by properly qualified auditors. (Very small cooperative societies with a turnover less than £5,000, fewer than 500 members and assets below £5,000 may appoint two unqualified auditors.)

Both societies and companies must file annual returns, including their audited accounts, with their respective Registrar. For societies, the accounting year coincides with the calendar year and returns must be lodged within three months unless special dispensation for a different accounting period or a deferred return is obtained from the Registrar of Friendly Societies. For companies the accounting year may be selected by the founding members and notified to the Registrar (often it is stated in the articles of association) otherwise it will correspond to the government year ending 31 March. The annual return must be completed within ten months of the end of the financial year. In all cases the annual audited accounts must be presented to and approved by the annual general meeting of all members.

Winding-up

There are three ways of having a cooperative wound up:

□ *Members' voluntary liquidation.* This is carried out by resolution of the members who appoint a liquidator to complete the procedure. The enterprise must be solvent and have paid or be able to pay all outstanding debts within one year.

□ *Creditors' voluntary liquidation.* If the enterprise is not solvent then the members can pass the winding up resolution, in which case the creditors will appoint the liquidator.

□ *Compulsory liquidation.* The court has the power to order an enterprise to be wound up whether or not it is solvent. Any member, qualified creditor or the Registrar can instigate the action. This is most likely to occur when the enterprise becomes insolvent and a creditor decides that enough is enough.

There is also a procedure available to cooperative societies called an *instrument of dissolution* procedure. This is similar to a members' voluntary liquidation but requires all liabilities to be settled within three months.

Registration of cooperative societies can be cancelled by the Registrar if membership falls below the minimum of seven persons required by law.

Before taking such an irrevocable step as winding-up, any cooperative group should have consulted their legal and financial advisers to establish that winding-up is the most sensible course of action in the particular circumstances.

Key questions and practical steps

Before you select a legal structure and go ahead with forming your cooperative, you must decide:

□ The name of your cooperative.
□ Your aims and objectives.

❑ What you are intending to do by way of trading or other activity to achieve your aims and objectives.

❑ Who will be the members of the cooperative.

❑ Who will make up the directors/management committee and how many they will be.

❑ (If a community cooperative) whether you want to try and obtain charitable status.

❑ What will happen to any profits.

❑ What will happen to the assets if the cooperative closes down.

Once these questions have been settled, your group will be able to select the model constitution nearest to what you want. Study the model you choose (or two or three) carefully and decide if you want to make changes. Don't be put off by the legal language; it is not as daunting as it first appears and most of the bodies promoting the various models provide explanatory notes (see Appendix 1)[2]. Remember that it is easier to adapt a memorandum and articles of association than it is to change a rule in a cooperative society model rules. Once model rules have been accepted and registered the Registrar is unenthusiastic about adaptations and still allowing the reduced fee payable when model rules are used.

The fee for registering a cooperative society with model rules was £115 in August 1983, although this changes from time to time. The fee is £250 when a set of new rules and not model rules is used. The current fee for registering a company is £50. (If there is share capital, capital duty may be payable.)

Registering a cooperative society is a matter of completing the blanks in the chosen model rules and the necessary forms and sending them off to

---

2. The booklet *How to set up a Worker Cooperative* published by the National Cooperative Development Agency includes copies of the relevant forms and notes for registering both cooperatives and companies. (See Appendix 2.)

the Registrar of Friendly Societies. The promoting bodies (see Appendix 1) provide detailed information about what to do together with copies of the appropriate forms to be completed. The services of a lawyer are not required.

Small adaptations to the detail of a model constitution can be made without legal assistance, but it is important to make sure that the changes you propose are acceptable to the Registrar before you type your final version and complete the forms. If you want any substantive changes make sure you know what they are and then obtain legal advice. Remember, however, that lawyers are often very ignorant about cooperatives and few have any experience of dealing with them. By that stage you will probably know more than the lawyer about the possible legal structures for cooperatives!

Registering a company using a model memorandum and articles of association can be as simple as filling in the blanks, completing the necessary forms and sending them all off with the fee to the Registrar of Companies. The services of a lawyer are not necessary although a lawyer or JP has to sign as a witness of the signing of the application forms and papers.

For a community company that wishes to obtain charitable status it is essential to make sure that your proposed memorandum and articles of association are acceptable for charitable status before you incorporate the company. Although charitable status can be given after incorporation only, the Inland Revenue (in Scotland) or the Charity Commissioners (in England and Wales) will indicate if your proposed constitution is acceptable or if not, how it must be changed. If you register your company first and then find you need to make changes in order to acquire charitable status you will need to go through the process of extraordinary general meetings to make a constitutional change. While that is not difficult for a company with a small membership it can be confusing for the existing and prospective members.

Chapter 8

Management and Human Relations

Ownership and membership

The owners of a cooperative are its members and it is the members together in a general meeting who exert ultimate control over the enterprise. Whatever management and organisational structures are created, the managers derive their authority from the members and they are ultimately responsible and accountable to them.

Membership of a cooperative therefore carries certain responsibilities and obligations. Working for a workers' cooperative should be more than having a job, it should mean assuming some of the worry and concern that goes with ownership. Your livelihood depends on the collective endeavours of all your colleagues. Membership of a community cooperative implies a decision to work with others for the common good and to devote energy and skills to the benefit of all. The cooperative group which has thought through what it wants to achieve and aims at an agreed set of goals is more likely to succeed than a disunited group uncertain of where it is going. Because the commitment required of members is considerable, it is important to allow people, especially prospective new members, the chance to gain some prior understanding of the cooperative and to judge whether they wish to adopt the cooperative cause.

A preamble to a cooperative's constitution provides a statement of ideals and objectives with which all members should be expected to agree. It follows that a certain commitment comes from that agreement. The Scott Bader Commonwealth took that process a stage further when they adopted in 1972 a *Code of Practice for Members* that spells out in some detail how they hope to work together and relate to the outside world. It is reproduced below.

Scott Bader Commonwealth

A We recognise that we are first a working community and that it is our basic attitude to our work and to our fellow workers that gives life and meaning to the Commonwealth.

B We have agreed that as a community our work involves four tasks, economic, technical, social and political, neglect of any one of which will in the long term diminish the Commonwealth. We feel that the practical working out of a balance between the four tasks is a continuing study for the membership as a whole.

C We are conscious of a common responsibility to share our work among ourselves in such a way that it becomes a meaningful and creative part of our lives rather than merely as a means to an end.

D We recognise that there are some members in a position of authority. Such members have a greater opportunity and hence a special responsibility to facilitate the building of jobs which are capable of fulfilling us as people; to act as 'catalysts of common effort' and not as authoritarian 'bosses'.

E We recognise that since management by consent rather than coercion is an appropriate style for the Company, a corresponding effort to accept responsibility is required from us all. This will show in a desire to attend meetings and to participate in the affairs of our community; it will show in increased communication between person and person and between groups and departments; it will show in an effort to understand the problems encountered and the contribution made by those in other areas of our organisation; above all it will be seen as a genuine willingness to learn, to develop and grow.

F We try to be open and frank in our relationships with our fellow workers, to face difficulties rather than avoid them and to solve problems by discussion and agreement rather than through reference to a third party.

G We are agreed that in the event of a downturn in trade we will share all remaining work rather than expect any of our fellow members to be deprived of employment, even if this requires a reduction in earnings by all.

H We have agreed not to hold second jobs if our doing

so is likely to deprive others (in the community at large) of employment or to affect our interest at work adversely.

I We are agreed that, as the foundation of our Commonwealth abolished here the power of share ownership, we shall strive to discourage our money from being used to profit from other people's work or to control other people's lives.

J We recognise that we have a responsibility to the society in which we live and believe that where we have some special talent or interest we should offer this to the wider community. Thus most of us are engaged in some form of social, political or public service, however small.

K We are agreed that (in addition to such disinterested services that we offer as individuals) our social responsibility extends to:

1 Limiting the products of our labour to those beneficial to the community, in particular excluding any products for the specific purpose of manufacturing weapons of war.

2 Reducing any harmful effect of our work on the natural environment by rigorously avoiding the negligent discharge of pollutants.

3 Questioning constantly whether any of our activities are unnecessarily wasteful of the earth's natural resources.

L As members of the Commonwealth we support the basic ideas expressed in the Preamble to the Constitution and reaffirm that the Commonwealth stands for a new approach to the problems of work and society. Therefore we accept that commitment to the principles of the Commonwealth implies an active concern for the expression of these principles both in our working lives and in the other areas of our lives.

Adopted at a General Meeting
held on the 19th day of July 1972

Management structures

The cooperative enterprise is not run by all members meeting together daily. All cooperative enterprises must establish a management structure to ensure that the day-to-day business of taking decisions happens efficiently and that the enterprise does what is necessary to succeed. There is a distinction between ultimate control of the membership and the authority vested in the management structure, but at all times the management remains accountable to the membership. Even small worker cooperatives who manage their affairs on a very democratic collective basis find it necessary to define areas of responsibility and daily decision-making (in other words to create a management structure) if their enterprise is to operate at all efficiently.

In most community and larger worker cooperatives the management jobs and management structure are not very different from any other business. People with management, sales, financial and business organisation skills are hired by the enterprise to run and develop it. In smaller cooperatives as in any small business, the members find themselves having to do everything, from practical 'on the job' work to the various management tasks.

Boards, committees and the community

A cooperative society is run by a committee of management and a cooperative company by a board of directors (sometimes called a council of management). The committee/board members are elected or appointed at the annual general meeting. Most model legal structures provide for only some of the committee/board members to retire each year so as to ensure some continuity. At the annual general meeting the annual audited accounts and a report on the activities of the year are presented to the members. The AGM is the once a year opportunity laid down by law for the members to find out what is going on. Of course, most cooperatives will find other means of keeping members in touch during the year and if there are especially important decisions to make in the meantime an extraordinary general meeting (EGM) can be arranged.

The committee/board is responsible for managing the enterprise and taking policy and executive decisions within the overall framework laid down by the full membership. Most committees/boards meet at least once a month but may require to meet more often. Day-to-day management is delegated to a manager (or whatever management structure the cooperative evolves) although in the early days of a cooperative when it is small all the members may act as the committee/directors and make decisions on daily running themselves. That is good at that stage because it enables all concerned to become fully involved in a process which might well be new to many, if not all members. But if that concentration on detail continues once the enterprise has a working management two drawbacks soon become obvious:

1. The committee's/board's attention is directed away from its real purpose: deciding policy and monitoring progress.
2. The committee/board is making decisions about matters which are really the responsibility of the managers and particular workers. Managers can see this as 'interference' and resent it, so not give of their best.

Some cooperatives encourage ordinary members or workers to attend committee/board meetings (strictly speaking as observers although the informality of many cooperatives easily permits 'participative observation') so they can keep in touch with what is being planned and decided.

The committee/board will have a chairperson or convener who is also chairperson of the cooperative, and a vice-chair. There will be a cooperative or company secretary who is responsible for making sure all the legal obligations are met: these include making the annual return to the Registrar, ensuring that the annual general meeting is held at the proper time and that the society/company keeps to its proper procedures as laid down in the rules/articles of association. There will probably be a treasurer who is responsible for making sure that the cooperative's accounts are properly kept and that the finances are in good order.

The treasurer will not usually do the book-keeping (at least once the cooperative is running smoothly) as that is a job done 'in the office' by the working management, but he/she will oversee what is done.

Subcommittees will sometimes be appointed to concentrate on particular aspects of the cooperative's work: these might be, for example, specific business areas, personnel, or finance.

The committee/board is also responsible for ensuring that the cooperative meets its objectives, both commercial and social. That can be a difficult and delicate balancing act as commercial and social aspects can conflict and hard choices and decisions require to be taken.

It can sometimes be hard to maintain good communication between the committee/board and the members to whom they are responsible. Even in a worker cooperative where the members are involved actively on a day-to-day basis a gap can still develop between the workers and the committee. The workers find themselves just doing a job and not knowing much about the cooperative's affairs. The committee and/or the managers may be tempted to keep their information to themselves and they find that holding on to information can be a means of retaining and exercising power. Although cooperation is about the democratic organisation of work and mutual sharing, it is all too easy for workers and managers in a cooperative enterprise to revert to the traditional styles of behaviour. It takes constant effort and thought to try and make the cooperative way work.

In the community cooperative there is a triangular problem of communication and involvement between community, board and management, and workers. It can be too easy for local people to lose track of what their cooperative business is doing and for the committee/board to make the maintenance of flow of information a low priority. That can lead to feelings of mistrust and suspicion which prevent the community members from appreciating the very real problems of setting up and running the cooperative and to the board closing in on itself and resenting 'interference' and criticism.

In short, the participation implied in a cooperative does not just happen – it has to be an important priority of those involved. That means finding time to make sure people know what is happening, arranging extra general meetings, producing newsletters and magazines, talking to groups of people locally and with all the members of the cooperative enterprise itself.

Cooperative managers

Managing a cooperative is a particularly difficult job. It is the manager who has to balance the aspirations of the workers as owners with the business realities which face those same workers as the employees of the cooperative. The manager of a community cooperative has to balance the social aspirations of the members with the commercial realities of running the business activities and creating genuine jobs for local people.

In smaller worker cooperatives which are collectively organised, everybody is in a sense a manager. The general rule in larger worker and community cooperatives is that someone is appointed manager. Sometimes that person emerges from the membership but it is often the case that management skills are missing from the initiating group and so a manager has to be recruited.

Hiring a manager can be one of the most important tasks undertaken by a cooperative because a good manager is a key to the success of the business. If a tradesman does a bad job it is serious enough, but all that is affected is the immediate work. If a manager is incompetent, then the whole business will suffer. Because of the nature of management tasks, the fact that someone is incompetent is not always immediately apparent. The longer it takes to discover incompetence the worse the potential effect on the business.

First make out a *job description* which lists what the manager will have to do. The preparation of this list will itself make you aware of the management needs of your cooperative. Then make up a *job specification* which describes the kind of person you are looking for, their personality, skills and previous experience. What you will end up with is probably a description of some amazing super-person and so it is usually necessary to go through description and specification again trying to be realistic about what you can expect. An all too common problem is to expect too much of a manager: they are only one part of what should be a team.

Interviewing is difficult: there is no magic formula in making an assessment and an awful lot can depend on hunch and 'gut-feeling'. The interviewing panel should discuss not only what they are looking for but how they will run the interview and who will ask what questions. A two-stage interview is often quite useful with stage one giving candidates the chance to see around the enterprise and the local area and to chat informally to members and workers. It is important that the candidates for a manager's job in a cooperative, whether worker or community, know what they are letting themselves in for.

Having interviewed, only decide to appoint someone if you are certain he/she is the right person. If you are not certain it is far better to make no appointment and re-advertise rather than risk making the wrong choice. Always take up references and telephone the referees if you are not sure about some aspect and want to follow it up. It is often not what references say that is important but what they don't say, and referees can be more open 'off the record' on the telephone than in writing.

Once management staff have been appointed in a cooperative it is important that their role is clear both to them and to everybody else. They must know what their reponsibilities are, to whom they report and to whom they should go for advice and consultation. At the same time the cooperative must know what it expects of its manager(s) and have a means of monitoring his/her progress. If things go wrong, and it is perfectly possible that they will, then it is far better to take a decision sooner rather than later to change the manager, no matter how painful acting on that decision might be. Part of the responsibility of cooperative ownership is not only to hire, but also to fire if needs be.

Hiring . . .

Hiring and firing in a cooperative enterprise are not simple matters. Hiring means finding the right people for the job: not only must they be capable of doing the work task, but they must also fit into the working environment and agree with and adopt the particular cooperative's philosophy. Most people applying for a job are not expecting to find a philosophy along with it, so time must be found for them to understand the nature of the enterprise with which they may become associated.

Particular problems can be experienced when new workers/members are added to the founding group which will already have a common understanding, a way of working together, a bond developed through experiences good and bad, will have worked out their aims and objectives together, and have an intimate knowledge of their cooperative's affairs. Just one new member can upset existing relationships and challenge working practices. Questions can be resented and information held back. Confidence takes time to build up.

The process of hiring needs careful thought and attention to both the actual job on offer and the interviewing procedure. A job specification and job description should be prepared for all jobs to be filled. Remember that in a cooperative, particularly a small one which is building up, every worker is a key worker.

All employees working 16 hours or more per week must be given a written statement or a written contract of employment. This should show:

- ☐ The name of the employer and of the employee.
- ☐ The date when employment began.
- ☐ If any employment with a previous employer counts as part of continuous employment (for example, if the cooperative has been formed to follow on from a previous enterprise). If the employment is for a fixed term the expiry date must be given.
- ☐ The rate of pay, how paid and how often paid.
- ☐ The hours of work.
- ☐ Holiday entitlement.
- ☐ Any additional sick pay which may be paid.
- ☐ Pension arrangements.
- ☐ Length of notice required.
- ☐ The employee's job title (simply 'cooperative worker' will do).
- ☐ Any disciplinary and grievance rules and procedures.
- ☐ The person to whom the employee can apply if he is dissatisfied with any disciplinary decision.

. . . and firing

The corollary to hiring is firing. It is essential that any cooperative enterprise is clear about who or which body is entitled to dismiss a worker and that a clear procedure for handling grievances and disciplinary matters is established and clearly understood. Firing people in an enterprise which stands for participation and involvement can be especially difficult. There can be a reluctance to admit that the wrong person has been hired, or to face up to the fact that a working colleague is just not capable or suitable. It is understandably hard to deprive someone of their living, especially when the enterprise exists to do the best for its members and workers. Nonetheless firing has to be faced up to and the harsh decision sometimes taken. At such times a clear and set procedure can make a difficult process somewhat less personal.

Where anything other than a summary dismissal is concerned the following procedure of warnings may be used:

(a) In the case of minor 'offences' the individual should be given a formal oral warning or, if more serious, a written warning.
(b) Further misconduct within a specified period (say three months) should result in a further written warning with a set review date.
(c) Further misconduct within the set period would lead to a final warning that one repetition will result in dismissal.

In cases of serious misconduct which need investigation pending any action – for example, summary dismissal – an alternative is to suspend the individual concerned on full pay.

It is essential to be clear who can instigate the disciplinary procedure. Where there is a formal management structure then it will likely be the manager or a supervisor. In a less formal cooperative, it can be hard sometimes to raise questions of misconduct unless there is a recognised time and process for doing so – perhaps at a monthly general meeting. In the case of community and larger worker cooperatives it is common to set up a small staff affairs subcommittee within the board/committee of management to handle both disciplinary and grievance procedures.

The grievance procedure sets out how an individual can take up a complaint against the cooperative. Again it is important that the process is clear and understood. In the larger worker cooperatives most workers will be told to whom they should refer in the first instance and there will then be the chance to refer, perhaps through another level, eventually to the board or committee of management representing the whole cooperative. In the case of the smaller, informal cooperative the problem is more usually how to raise a grievance with colleagues who are also friends and where there is no clearly recognised management structure. In such situations it is vital, as with disciplinary questions, that the group finds an acceptable way in a general meeting of raising grievances when they are still insignificant 'niggles' rather than allow them to develop into major issues.

In small firms employing 20 people or less, individuals who have been employed full time (ie more than 16 hours per week) for two years are covered by unfair dismissal legislation (one year in larger companies). Part-timers working between eight and 16 hours only qualify after five years. The legislation allows individuals to file a complaint with the industrial tribunal within three months of dismissal and the tribunal can, if they uphold the complaint, order reinstatement or (where that is not practicable) compensation. The best way to safeguard against unfair dismissal complaints is to have good procedures for disciplinary action and grievances, and to make sure that all decisions are properly recorded in the minutes of meetings and copies of all correspondence properly kept. Any one who is dismissed after six months' employment is entitled to a letter stating the reasons for dismissal.

Employment policy

An employment policy is a further important area for discussion. Worker cooperatives are established sometimes with the specific purpose of creating employment for a particular group of people or in a particular locality. One of the strengths of the worker cooperative in local terms is that it is rooted in a community and therefore less likely to consider relocating. Any policy about who to employ has to be carefully balanced with the business needs of the enterprise.

That balance is especially difficult for the community cooperative which is set up with the particular object of creating employment for the people of a given locality.

☐ Will the cooperative concentrate on employing local people? What will happen when the best person for a job comes from outside?
☐ Will the cooperative concentrate on employing only *unemployed* local people or (as with most private businesses) will it favour people already in a job on the grounds that they are productive sooner than someone who has been out of work for a long time?
☐ What level of training will the cooperative try and provide?
☐ Will the cooperative attempt to 'rehabilitate' its workers, tolerating in the meantime the various problems (bad time-keeping for example) that will arise?

An employment policy of social benefit increases the costs to the business, making profitability more difficult. Likewise the provision of social facilities, creches, generous maternity and paternity leave, flexible holidays and other desirable benefits puts pressure on the economic viability of the cooperative. A persistent dilemma is to steer a course which maximises the social benefit without jeopardising the business viability.

Disabled staff
Businesses with more than 20 employees are required to include a quota of 3 per cent of registered disabled people. The Disablement Resettlement Officer (contact through the local Jobcentre) can advise and help you find suitable disabled people.

Health and safety

The health and safety legislation puts a legal responsibility on all employers to make sure that their business is a safe place to work: that includes premises, plant, machinery, procedures and systems and also the effect on the environment. There is also a requirement to provide instruction, training and supervision to ensure health and safety at work.

Businesses with more than five workers must have a written health and safety policy which should spell out the various safety arrangements and procedures and the responsibilities and duties of all concerned in the business.

The legislation is enforced by the Health and Safety Commission for industrial businesses or by the local Environmental Health Officer for retail and service businesses. These officers have wide-ranging powers of entry and inspection and can instruct that certain practices are changed in order to be made safe, prohibit the use of equipment or machinery which is considered dangerous and, in extreme cases, prosecute the business or individuals within it. Likewise individual employees can sue their employers for negligence.

The Employers' Liability (Compulsory Insurance) Act 1969 prescribes that all employers must insure against liability for personal injury and disease sustained by employees in the course of their work.

All cooperatives will want to provide good working conditions, but there is always a temptation to skimp on safety, to take risks, short-cut a procedure, use a piece of equipment known to be faulty, particularly when the pressure is on or when workers are tired. Once the accident has happened it is too late. Preventive action is the best way of reducing accidents. A written policy statement ensures that cooperative members consider the problem and think about their methods and machinery from a safety point of view. Appointing a safety sub-committee – even if only a committee of one – means that someone is always thinking about safety and can raise points which others may not notice.

Trades unions

Some people assume that trade unionism has no part to play in cooperatives because the whole concept of cooperative endeavour does away with the need for the traditional role of the trade union in that work-force, management and owners are joined in a common task. This view is an over-simplification and overlooks important functions for the organised labour movement within the cooperative sector of the economy. However, these functions *are* different in emphasis and style from the trade union role in the normal economy and call for changed attitudes from trade unionists.

Cooperatives are businesses with a work-force. Fair pay and good conditions remain an important question on which the relevant trade union can advise and ensure that cooperatives are aware of accepted practice in other sectors. It is unlikely that trade union wage negotiation will be relevant in a cooperative which should have its own demo-cratic consultative procedures. However, the trade union nationally negotiated rates are a yardstick against which cooperatives can measure their pay and conditions. The machinery for trade union negotiation can be used as a procedure to fall back on if internal procedures fail, this being especially relevant for community cooperatives where a divergence of interest can emerge between com-munity members and workers.

No cooperative democracy – indeed no democra-tic system – works simply because it exists. Those who make up the system and play a part in it have to be prepared to work for its success. It is not difficult for a small group to exert undue influence or indeed control on an apparently democratic organisation. The withholding of important infor-mation can place some members at a dis-advantage and conversely, the possession of certain information or skills can give some members a powerful advantage. If a democratic system is not working properly there needs to be a method for aggrieved members to seek changes. It is here that a role could lie for the trades unions: that of acting as independent representatives of labour who can take action if any one cooperative democracy seems to any group of its members to be operating properly no longer. Such a role – almost a watchdog role – could be important but it requires of the trades union movement a strong commitment to promoting the cooperative sector in the economy.

The satisfactions of cooperating

The first practical objective of a worker or community cooperative is to create and sustain jobs for its own members and local residents. The return on investment which a cooperative seeks is first measured in terms of securing the livelihood of the people in the business and second in terms of developing and strengthening that business. A primary satisfaction is that the effort which goes into creating the business is returned as benefit for the workers and local people and not as distributed profit to external shareholders.

The cooperative, being owned and controlled by its members, can determine its own priorities and its own path of development. Because it must survive in the market place, compete with other firms, and borrow money from traditional sources, the cooperative inevitably finds itself restricted in various ways, but the final decisions rest nonetheless with the members. The cooperative does not have to pursue maximum profit levels if it prefers not to. It can adopt the working practices it prefers provided they do not threaten its commercial survival.

Because the cooperative is controlled by its membership and because of its links with the area in which it is based, it is more securely fixed as a part of the local economic infrastructure. Whereas the owners of a private concern might be attracted by offers of takeover or inducements to expand elsewhere, cooperative owners have a commitment to their homes, their families and other local people.

The cooperative structure and ethos ensure that profits are used primarily for the development of the business. Thereafter they might be applied for community benefit and/or as a bonus to workers.

In all events, profits are ploughed back into the local economy and not siphoned off elsewhere. The principle of mutual endeavour and mutual help can be found in all aspects.

Ideally the cooperative is a business in which the working conditions and environment are tailored to the needs and wishes of the work-force. That is not to say that pay and conditions are not constrained by the harsh realities of commercial survival: they are. Nor is it to suggest that cooperatives escape management worker conflicts: they don't. Boring jobs are still boring in a cooperative. But one purpose of the cooperative is to make working conditions as good as possible and, perhaps most important, working members themselves have a say in what the priorities should be and how scanty resources might be used.

Of itself the cooperative structure does not create democracy nor does it ensure participation: it does however provide the framework for democratic ways of working, for participation and thus for a healthy, open working environment. Filling in the framework requires hard work, careful and sensitive human relations and a realisation that most people in our society have been brought up not to work cooperatively. Competition and individual assertion are the bench-marks of education and commercial success in the western world, not mutual assistance and cooperative endeavour. In this regard cooperatives are struggling against decades (centuries?) of tradition and practice.

There is therefore something of the pioneer's excitement in setting up and running a cooperative. You are doing something about which others are, to say the least, sceptical. Additionally there is the excitement of running a business, doing something that sells, seeing a plan come to fruition, seeing people work together, and earning a living for yourself with other equal partners. It can be worrying, it will be hard, tempers will fray, but if you succeed what a magnificent feeling!

If you fail – and there are bound to be failures – there will be heartache, personal financial hard-

145

ship perhaps, strained personal relationships, and a feeling of emptiness. But without failures there could be no successes because nobody would risk anything. The fear of failure should not be allowed to stand in the way of new attempts to create enterprises and jobs.

Chapter 9

Premises — and Other Things

Finding premises

Finding suitable premises can be difficult, especially when small-scale workshops are sought for starting up or when premises are wanted in or near areas of high unemployment such as in a large housing estate. Many small workshops have been lost through redevelopment in the past 20 years and local planning regulations can prevent business developments in residential areas (often just where they are most required).

Until recently most public authority factory building concentrated on large (upwards of 10,000 sq ft) advance units which were part of the policy of attracting new 'footloose' industry into areas of high unemployment. The last few years have seen a marked change in both public and private sector: most authorities are now building factory units of 5,000 sq ft or less and the more adventurous are experimenting with 'work yards' and multi-occupied conversions of large buildings.

First enquiries for premises should be made through the local authorities: both district and county or regional and the new town corporations. In addition to having their own commercial and industrial property for leasing, local authorities also own disused property (eg schools and clinics) which can often be acquired by a cooperative enterprise at little or no cost or on special rental terms. Officials in the Planning Department often know about privately owned empty property and can suggest which properties a cooperative group might investigate.

Regional industrial development organisations such as the Scottish and Welsh Development Agencies, the Highlands and Islands Development Board, the Development Board for Rural Wales and, in England, CoSIRA and the English Industrial Estates Corporation have extensive factory building programmes which increasingly recognise the need for small factories. They can offer rent-free periods and other assistance in certain circumstances.

Other places to look for premises are the local papers and estate agents. Major companies in the district, public corporations (for example British Rail) and major owners of buildings and land can sometimes help. There is nothing to beat using your eyes and ears as you walk about the locality to find something suitable and then tracking down the owner.

Managed workspaces

One type of premises-based development which has become quite common is a large old building – for example a former school or a disused factory – converted into a number of small workspaces for separate businesses. At one level such a workspace is simply a multi-occupied industrial or commercial building. At another it becomes a working community with a range of services organised by the management with the costs shared pro rata on space rented by the tenant businesses. The common services might include security, reception, typing, toilets, meeting rooms, cleaning of common areas, background heat, telephone system, janitorial services, building maintenance and so forth. Tenants pay a charge which covers both rent and services, leaving the workspace management to look after the building. Individual workspaces are normally small and sometimes flexible in size with demountable partitions. Tenancies are on an easy-in easy-out basis which means the newly started enterprise can take space without encumbering itself with any long-term leases or rental agreements.

The workspace environment is ideal for newly started enterprises. The bother of looking after a building is removed and so is much of the day-to-day hassle, leaving the people running the business free to do just that. Within a workspace which develops as a working community there is usually a deal of inter-trading, and that in turn leads to mutual support and assistance when things seem difficult. When common problems can be discussed, things do not seem so daunting. A further dimension of the workspace is the provision by the workspace company of business advice and information together with basic business services: typing, copying, message taking, even book-keeping.

A number of community cooperatives and businesses have begun to establish workspaces in their areas, seeing them both as a way of bringing new enterprises and thus jobs into the locality and as a means of providing the resources and environment needed to aid the establishment of other cooperative enterprises. A good example of a community-run workspace is Govan Workspace Ltd in Glasgow (see page 34).

Local enterprise workshops

One problem facing a community cooperative in an area of high unemployment is that of encouraging local people to come up with ideas for enterprise. A number of community cooperative groups have drawn up plans to create a Local Enterprise Workshop (LEW) to help stimulate this process. One such is Forgewood Enterprises Ltd, Motherwell (see page 41) who are establishing theirs in some empty houses which are the property of the district council.

An LEW provides space where local people can meet and tinker with ideas for products, store equipment and materials, and from which they can develop and try out their business idea.

149

Extremely small workshops are also available for rent. The LEW needs a basic range of tools and equipment for certain selected trades (knitting machines and woodworking tools in Forgewood), is open for as many hours as needed each week and has supervisors on duty to give practice advice and guidance. The LEW will also act as a centre for evening classes on setting up and running a business and for skill training workshops. Through the LEW local people will be able to meet and consult various experts from helping agencies about legal and accountancy problems, raising finance, marketing and so on.

Planning permission

If you are changing the use of your premises from their former purpose then you may need 'change of use' planning permission and should consult the Planning Department of the local district council. Any change to the outside of a building - even putting up a sign - also requires planning permission.

If you carry out any significant building works you are likely to require a building warrant from the Building Control Officer of the local district council even where planning permission was not required. If you are uncertain, it is best to enquire rather than run into problems later on.

Security

Keeping premises secure is a continuing - and growing - problem especially in larger urban areas. The local police crime prevention officer will give advice on what to do (and what to avoid) and then it is a question of striking the best balance between the ideal and the resources at your disposal.

Fire prevention

If you carry out alterations which have required a

building warrant and/or planning permission, then you will probably have had automatic contact with the fire prevention officer. If not, it is worth consulting him, via the local fire station, for advice based on his experience of fire risks and dangers.

Business administration

Telephone
Remember to order your telephone system as soon as you can. Although business is given priority over private installations, there can sometimes be a considerable waiting period. Consider also whether to have an answering device installed if you need to be able to take messages at all hours but cannot guarantee to have someone on duty by the phone.

Insurance
All businesses are required by law to take out employer's liability insurance. This covers the cooperative against any claims from an employee becoming injured or ill through working for the enterprise. It is also necessary to take out public liability insurance if there is even a slight chance of third parties becoming injured or ill because of the activities of your business, or of their property being lost or damaged. Local authorities are particularly insistent that companies which do work for them have public liability insurance.

Depending on your type of business, it is advisable to take out other insurance cover, notably on your premises and the contents. It is best to consult a reputable insurance broker about this and other cover which may be relevant to your enterprise.

Copyright
Copyright covers literature, computer software, crafts, music and other forms of creation and exists to prevent people from copying another's

work without payment. Basically copyright always belongs to the creator, unless there is a specific other agreement with another person. Thus where a piece of work is commissioned, the copyright can belong to the client and likewise, if a writer or painter is regularly employed his/her copyright can be forfeited to the employer.

Patents
Registering a patent aims to prevent the unlawful copying of the way an invented article works rather than how it looks. It is quite a complex process both legally and technically to register a patent and the normal course is to consult and make use of a registered patent agent. Enquire first at your nearest Small Firms Information Centre.

Trade marks
Registering the name of your product or service as a registered trade mark prevents others from using it. Registration is with the Patents Office and it is easiest to use the services of a patent agent. Enquire first at your nearest Small Firms Information Centre.

Distribution
The main methods of sending goods within the UK are by post, rail or road haulage; it all depends on what you have to send and its weight and bulk. It is worth checking the relative prices, speed and convenience of all methods before deciding. If you are a regular user it is sometimes possible to negotiate a special rate. Post and rail enquiries should start at your nearest main post office/railway parcels office; road haulage starts in the Yellow Pages.

Business stationery
Every registered cooperative or company must have proper business stationery which displays its name, registered address and registration number. The word 'Limited' can only be used by a business

which has limited liability through incorporation as a company or as a cooperative.

Public relations

Publicity and public relations are usually seen as part of the selling process: publicity is free advertising. However, for cooperatives, publicity and public relations are important in developing the image of cooperatives in the public eye. To many people cooperatives signify the Coop store in the High Street, or something rather cranky, if not downright doubtful, even unbusinesslike and disorganised. Every new cooperative - community and worker - represents a growing movement to create a cooperative sector in the economy. Any chance to promote and expound what they are doing is a chance to extend public interest in co-operation and to correct misunderstandings and misconceptions.

Appendix 1
Sources of Help and Advice

For the group setting up a cooperative enterprise there appears to be a maze of agencies and organisations devoted to giving information, advice and assistance, and it can be a daunting problem to decide just where to start. For many people, entering the world of business and commerce means learning a new language.

The starting point for each group will depend on what they need and where they are. The resources available vary according to district and this section aims to clarify what agencies exist, what they aim to offer, and how to contact them. Each group will have to find out for itself what assistance it can draw on and must decide which national organisations to contact.

Information and advice are there for you to use. You will get conflicting advice. You will get good and bad advice. The final decision is yours; weigh up what you are told and make your own judgements. Don't follow advice blindly, but equally don't ignore what others say. The clearer you are in your own mind about what you want to do, the better you will be able to use the information, advice and help which others can offer. Inevitably a listing such as this concentrates on national, or at best regional, agencies and cannot include all local advisory or support organisations.

Agencies which specialise in cooperative development

Advisory
1. Cooperative Development Agency
Broadmead House, 21 Panton Street, London SW1Y 4DR; 01-839 2988

Government appointed national agency; worker coop model rules; neighbourhood coop model rules; link with local cdas; specialist business advice service.

2. Industrial Common Ownership Movement Ltd
7 Corn Exchange, Leeds LS1 7BP; 0532 461737
National membership body to promote common ownership; industrial coop model rules; industrial common ownership model memorandum and articles of association; an information exchange forum; advisory service; quarterly newsletter; some regional branches.

3. Cooperative Union Ltd
Holyoake House, 1 Hanover Street, Manchester M60 0AS; 061–832 4300

95 Morrison Street, Glasgow G5 8LP; 041–429 2556
National advisory and information organisation of established coop movement; advisory service.

4. Scottish Cooperatives Development Committee Ltd
Templeton Business Centre, Templeton Street, Bridgeton, Glasgow G40 1DA; 041-554 3797
Main Scottish advisory and development organisation for worker coops; advisory service throughout Scotland, local staff in Clydeside, Highlands and Aberdeen; model memorandum and articles of association; marketing service.

5. Community Business Scotland
39 Vicar Street, Falkirk; 0324 38458
Scottish federation to link and promote community coops and businesses; quarterly newsletter; sponsors local advisory agency in Central Region.

6. Highlands and Islands Development Board
Bridge House, Bank Street, Inverness IV1 1QR; 0463 34171
Community coop support programme; advisory service, consultancy, loans and grants for small business.

7. Antur Broydd Cymru
(Welsh Community Enterprise), 3 Christina Street, Swansea, West Glamorgan; 0792 53498
Welsh federation to link and promote worker coops, community business and local development agencies; quarterly newsletter.

8. Wales Cooperative Development Training Centre
55 Charles Street, Cardiff CF1 4ED; 0222 372237
Independent advisory service for worker coops sponsored by Wales TUC.

9. Mid Wales Development
(Development Board for Rural Wales), Ladywell House, Newton, Powys SY16 1JB; 0686 26965
Business advice and assistance; factories; pound for pound grants for social projects within a multi-functional community coop; promotion of community coops including 50 per cent grant for cost of manager.

10. Northern Ireland Council of Cooperative Organisations
New University of Ulster, Coleraine, Co Londonderry; 0265 4141
Independent voluntary liaison and consultative body for various coop sectors.

11. Job Ownership Ltd
9 Poland Street, London W1V 3DG; 01-437 5511
Independent non-profit consultancy organisation; promotes individual capital contributions and asset sharing; draft model memorandum and articles of association.

12. Instant Muscle
c/o Rank Xerox (UK) Ltd, Cambridge House, Oxford Road, Uxbridge, Middlesex UB8 1HS; 0895 51166
National advisory service for young peoples' coops; model rules available.

13. Mutual Aid Centre
18 Victoria Park Square, London E2 9PF; 01-980 6263
Sponsors demonstration coop projects; research; publications.

Finance
14. Industrial Common Ownership Finance Ltd
4 St Giles Street, Northampton NN1 1AA; 0604 37563
National revolving loan fund for worker coops; runs local loan funds for local authorities; consultancy service for establishing loan funds and appraisal processes.

Training and Research
15. Beechwood College
Elmete Lane, Roundhay, Leeds LS8 2LQ; 0532 720205
Regular training courses for worker and community coops; publications; conference facilities.

16. The Plunkett Foundation for Cooperative Studies
31 St Giles, Oxford OX1 3LF; 0865 53960
Courses and seminars; publications; library facilities.

17. Cooperatives Research Unit
Faculty of Technology, Open University, Walton Hall, Milton Keynes MK7 6AA; 0908 653303
Research into coops; publications, including case study series; business games.

18. Commonwork Trust
Bore Place, Chiddingstone, Edenbridge, Kent TN8 7AR; 073277 255
Seminars and courses (in association with Cooperatives Research Unit); conference facilities.

19. Cooperative Studies Unit
Information service; training courses.

Official bodies and departments which either directly assist or are involved with new business formation

20. Department of Industry, Small Firms Division
Ashdown House, 123 Victoria Street, London SW1E 6RB;
01-212 8667, 8721, 6206
Network of Small Firms Information Centres (tel: freefone 2444) free information and signposting service; excellent free booklets on various aspects of business management; loan and grant schemes of government regional policy according to 'assisted area' status of each area.

21. Department of Employment
Contact local Jobcentres for help with recruitment of workers and information about training grants and training opportunities; about enterprise allowance scheme, the Community Programme and the Voluntary Projects Programme.

22. Manpower Services Commission
Moorfoot, Sheffield S1 4PQ; 0742 753275
Contact regional offices throughout Britain about Youth Training Scheme, Training Opportunities Programme, Community Programme and the Voluntary Projects Programme.

23. Scottish Development Agency
120 Bothwell Street, Glasgow G2 7JP; 041-248 2700

102 Telford Road, Edinburgh EH4 2NP; 031-343 1911
Consultancy assistance for worker coops through the SCDC; consultancy and advisory service, plus loan schemes, for small businesses; factories, including rent-free scheme; covers Scotland outside the Highlands and Islands.

24. Welsh Development Agency
Treforest Industrial Estate, Pontypridd, Mid Glamorgan CF37 5UT; 0443 852666
Consultancy and advisory service, plus loan schemes, for small businesses; factories, including rent-free scheme; serves Wales other than area covered by Development Board for Rural Wales (see 9. above).

25. Local Enterprise Development Unit
17-19 Linenhall Street, Belfast BT2 8AA; 0232 242582
Industrial coop adviser with particular remit for industrial and service coops; financial and advisory assistance for small businesses.

26. Council for Small Industries in Rural Areas (CoSIRA)
141 Castle Street, Salisbury SP1 3TP; 0722 36255

Advisory and loan service for very small firms in English non-urban areas; also some grant aid.

27. Scottish Agricultural Organisation Society Ltd
19 Claremont Crescent, Edinburgh EH7 4QD; 031-556 6574

Welsh Agricultural Organisation Society Ltd
PO Box 8, Aberystwyth, Dyfed SY23 1DR; 0970 4011
Development of and advisory service for agricultural and horticultural coops (especially marketing); model rules available.

28. Inland Revenue
Contact your local Inspector of Taxes to register for PAYE and find out where your Local Employers' Unit is for all necessary paperwork (PAYE and National Insurance).

Inland Revenue, Claims Branch, Trinity Park House, South Trinity Road, Edinburgh EH5 3SD; 031-552 6255
In Scotland charitable status is obtained through acceptance by the Inland Revenue Claims Branch.

29. Charity Commission
Head Office, 14 Ryder Street, London SW1Y 6AH; 01-214 6000

Graeme House, Derby Square, Liverpool L2 7SB; 051-227 3191
Northern register.

St Alban's House, 57-60 Haymarket, London SW1Y 4QX; 01-214 6000
Southern register.

30. HM Customs and Excise
VAT Administration Directorate, King's Beam House, Mark Lane, London EC3R 7HE; 01-626 1515
Contact local offices for information and advice about VAT registration.

31. Registrar of Companies
Companies House, Crown Way, Maindy, Cardiff CF4 3UZ; 0222 388588

102 George Street, Edinburgh EH2 3DJ; 031-225 5774

43-7 Chichester Street, Belfast BT1 4RJ; 0232 234121
Registration of companies.

32. Registrar of Friendly Societies
17 North Audley Street, London W1Y 2AP; 01-629 7001

58 Frederick Street, Edinburgh EH2 1NB; 031-226 3224

43-7 Chichester Street, Belfast BT1 4RJ; 0232 234121
Registration of coop societies.

33. Health and Safety Executive
25 Chapel Street, London NW1 5DT; 01-262 3277
Advice about requirements of Health and Safety at Work Act 1974; enforces legal requirements; local offices.

Health and Safety Commission
Regina House, 259 Old Marylebone Road, London NW1 5RR;
01-723 1262
Leaflets outlining the Act and information for employers,
employees and the self-employed.

Other relevant bodies

34. The Planning Exchange
186 Bath Street, Glasgow G2 4HG; 041-332 8541
Publish LEDIS (Local Economic Development Information
Service) and FRED (Financial Resources for Economic
Development).

35. Centre for Alternative Industrial and Technological Systems (CAITS)
Polytechnic of North London, Holloway Road, London
N7 8DB; 01-607 2789
Research and development of new product ideas; support for
coops; publish quarterly newsletter.

36. Institute for Workers' Control
Bertrand Russell House, Gamble Street, Nottingham
NG7 4ET; 0602 784504
Promotes workers' control mainly through trades union
movement; publishes regular bulletin.

37. Socialist Environment and Resources Association (SERA)
9 Poland Street, London W1V 3DG; 01-439 3749
Promotes cooperation as part of an alternative economic
strategy.

38. Centre for Employment Initiatives
140A Gloucester Mansions, Cambridge Circus, London
WC2H 8PA; 01-240 8901
Independent consultancy group which specialises in local
economic development, including community coops; publish
quarterly journal, *Initiatives*.

39. Charity Trading Advisory Group
9 Mansfield Place, London NW3 1HS; 01-794 9835
Advice on all aspects of charity trading.

40. Trades Union Congress
Congress House, Great Russell Street, London WC1B 3LS;
01-636 4030

Scottish TUC
Middleton House, 16 Woodlands Crescent, Glasgow G3 6DF;
041-332 4946

Wales TUC
Transport House, 1 Cathedral Road, Cardiff CF1 8SD; 0222
371495

The Irish Congress of Trade Unions
Northern Ireland Committee, 1-9 Castle Arcade, Belfast
BT1 5DG; 0232 241452
Contact the TUC or your local Trades Council for links with
relevant trades unions and trades unionists in your area.

41. Action Resource Centre
Henrietta House, 9 Henrietta Place, London W1M 9AG;
01-629 3826

Scottish Action Resource Centre
54 Shandwick Place, Edinburgh EH2 42T; 031-226 3669
Arrange secondments and other help from industry
especially for community-based projects.

42. Business in the Community
227A City Road, London EC1V 1JU; 01-253 3716

Scottish Business in the Community (Scot Bic)
25 St Andrew Square, Edinburgh EH1 2AF; 031-556 9761
Consortium of leading companies aiming to help meet needs
of local communities; promote establishment of local
enterprise agencies and trusts, in associaton with local
authorities; some practical and advisory help available.

43. Industry and Commerce
Many companies, not only those involved with ARC or BIC,
will assist economic development projects in their area.
Likewise organisations of business and commerce (eg
chambers of commerce, trades associations, Rotary, Lions
etc) can be worth contacting, especially for community-based
coops.

44. Cooperative Bank PLC
Business Development Manager, (Small Businesses and
Cooperatives), PO Box 101, 1 Balloon Street, Manchester
M60 4EP; 061-832 3456, exts 280, 282
Normal banking facilities and loans; contact local branch
managers or go direct to the advisory unit at the head office.

45. Trusts and foundations
A number of trusts and foundations are willing to help
economic development projects, more usually if they are
community based and with charitable status. Consult the
Directory of Grant-making Trusts. Obtain details of any local
trusts from the local district council chief executive or
administration department.

Local organisations and networks

46. Local Cooperative Development Agencies
Addresses of the network of local CDAs are available from
the national CDA or ICOM. For local contacts, ask the
district county or regional council. In Scotland worker coop
development is handled by the SCDC and there is a growing

regional network of community business development units
(contact Community Business Scotland – 5. above – for
details). Local CDAs arrange conferences and produce a
regular newsletter, *Coop Development News*. Further
information from the Cooperative Union (3. above).

47. Local Enterprise Trusts
LETs (or Agencies) are local groupings of business, local
authority and other interests formed to promote the
development of local small businesses, and to provide
information and advice, Local contacts from the district,
county or regional council or from Business in the
Community (42. above).

48. Local Authorities
Most local authorities have an industrial development,
economic development, or employment development unit.
This may be an independent mini-department, part of the
Planning Department or of the Chief Executive's
Department. If you don't know, start at the Chief Executive's
Department. Ask your district council and county or regional
council what they can do.

Local authorities offer a wide range of help to the
development of small businesses generally and of coops in
particular. This can include grants and loans, advice and
specialist consultancy, cheap or free premises, new enterprise
workshops/innovations centres, grants for development
agencies, rate relief for charities.

Appendix 2
Read All About It!

The books and publications listed in this section are divided into sections. Books published by an organisation listed in Appendix 1 are generally available direct from the organisation, whose reference number is given. Otherwise, they should be available through any reasonable bookshop. Most local cooperative development agencies run a book sales or lending service and local libraries should hold some of the titles listed. If they are not available at the library, you can always ask for them to be obtained.

General information about worker and community cooperation

These books provide some background and theoretical information about the ideas and practice of cooperation and cooperative development.

Community Business Works, Calouste Gulbenkian Foundation, 1982 (£2.00). Report by a working party set up to consider self-help groups and local productive activity; begins to establish a (very readable) theoretical framework for community economic activity.

Community Enterprise: British Potential and American Experience, Rosemary Newnham, University of Reading, 1981 (£2.50).

Polish Mondragon, Alastair Campbell, Scottish Cooperatives Development Committee, 1981 (90p) ref 4.

Producer Cooperatives in Eastern Europe: Lessons for the West, Alastair Campbell; Industrial Common-Ownership Movement; 1981 (90p) ref 2.

Worker-owners: The Mondragon Achievement, Alastair Campbell, Charles Keen, Geraldine Norman, Robert Oakeshott; Anglo-German Foundation, 1977 (£2.90). Good description of the Mondragon Group which has been an inspiration to many individuals and groups.

Workers Cooperatives: Jobs and Dreams, Jenny Thornley; Heinemann Educational Books, 1981 (£4.95). Critical look at worker cooperation in Britain; compared with development in France and Italy.

Forming a cooperative: the legal process

Community Business; a Model Constitution, Local Enterprise Advisory Project, 1984 (£2.50). A model memorandum and articles of association used extensively in Scotland and given charitable status; with notes.

Community Cooperatives: a Guide to a Working Constitution, Freer Spreckley, Beechwood, 1983 (£2.50) ref 15. A draft constitution for community coops; including social audit clauses.

Community Profit, Susan Wismer and David Pell, I.S. Five Press Toronto, 1981. Describes community-based economic development in Canada; and provides a good definition of what community economic development is and why it is important.

The Grassroots Developers, David Rock, The RIBA Conference Fund, 1980 (£3.50). A handbook for Town Development Trusts.

Industrial Common Ownership, David Watkins, Fabian Society, 1978 (65p).

LEAP Annual Reports 1978, 1979/80, 1980/81; 1981/82, Local Enterprise Advisory Project, Paisley College (50p, 50p, £1.00, £1.50). Accounts of the development of community business in practice and as an idea in the west of Scotland.

Our Own Resources, Roger Clarke, The Arkleton Trust, 1981 (£2.50). Cooperatives and community economic development in Canada.

The Self-Help Economy, Barry Knight and Ruth Hayes, London Voluntary Service Council, 1982 (£3.00). Social and economic development in the inner city; analyses nine projects in London with especial reference to the cost-effective use of public funds; recognises the value of the 'social profit'.

Social Audit, Freer Spreckley, Beechwood College publications, 1983 (£1.50) ref 15. A management tool for Cooperative Working; discusses the need for a social as well as a financial audit and suggests a model for carrying out a social enterprise audit.

Whose Business is Business? Calouste Gulbenkian
Foundation, 1981 (£3.50). Report of the Community Business
Ventures Unit; exhaustive survey of community and local
economic development initiatives in Britain.

*How to Convert a Company into an Industrial and Provident
Society*, Cooperative Development Agency, Information
Sheet, 1983 (free) ref 1. Brief details of the form of resolution
for adoption of industrial and provident society rules and
registration by the Registrar of Friendly Societies.

How to Form an Industrial Cooperative, Industrial Common
Ownership Movement (£10.50) ref 2. A complete guide to
setting up a worker coop using the ICOM model rules; kit
includes all the necessary forms for registration.

How to Set Up a Neighbourhood Cooperative, Cooperative
Development Agency, 1981 (£1.50) ref 1. A straightforward
guide to what a neighbourhood coop is, when and how to
form one; kit includes all the necessary forms for registration.

How to set up a Worker Cooperative, Cooperative
Development Agency, 1983 (£1.50) ref 1. Especially useful as
it contains copies of the ICOM model rules, the CDA model
rules for worker and neighbourhood coops, the ICOM model
memorandum and articles of association plus copies of all the
relevant leaflets and forms for registering coop societies and
companies.

Legal Structures for Cooperatives, John Fryer, Beechwood,
1981 (75p) ref 15. Useful outline of ICOM model rules, ICOM
memorandum and articles of association, CDA
neighbourhood coops and coop union model rules.

General guides to starting and running a cooperative enterprise

These titles give information and advice on both
the cooperative and the business aspects.

Community Business Information Kit, Local Enterprise
Advisory Project and Community Business Scotland, 1982
(£1.00). Ten straightforward information sheets plus single
sheet case-studies of various community businesses in
Scotland.

Community Cooperatives: a Guide, Highlands and Islands
Development Board, 1977 (£2.00) ref 6. The original guide
provided for local steering committees outlining what a
community coop is and the process of planning and
establishing one.

How to Start a Workers' Cooperative, Jim Brown,
Beechwood, 1981 (95p) ref 15. Good outline guide to planning
a coop enterprise.

Starting a Cooperative, John Lewis, Scottish Cooperatives Development Committee, 1979 (40p) ref 4. Checklist of points for a group thinking of setting up a coop.

Work-aid: Business Management for Cooperatives and Community Enterprises, Tony Naughton, Commonwork publications, 1981 (£2.95) ref 18. A very practical handbook covering all aspects of running and managing a small coop enterprise.

Workers' Cooperatives: a Handbook, Peter Cockerton, Tim Gilmour White, John Pearce, Anna Whyatt, Aberdeen Peoples Press, 1980 (available from SCDC, £3.95). Detailed description of what a workers' coop is, what needs to be considered when planning one and how to set it up using ICOM model rules.

Guides to setting up and running a small business

Business Start-up Guide, Scottish Development Agency, 1983 (free) ref 23. Useful introductory booklet explaining the various implications of going into business.

Creating Your Own Work, Micheline Mason, Gresham Books, 1980 (£1.25). Mixture of brief case studies and practical information.

Setting up a New Business, Maurice Gaffney, Department of Industry Small Firms Service (free) ref 20. One of a series of *free* information booklets. Others of particular value are *Marketing*, *Elements of book-keeping*, and *Employing people*.

The Small Business Guide, ed Colin Barrow, BBC Publications, 1982 (£4.50).

The Small Business Kit, D S Watkins and others, National Extension College, 1979 (£5.50). Comprehensive kit produced to go with TV programmes and later adapted for the 'Be Your Own Boss' series.

Starting Your Own Business, Consumers' Association, 1983 (£3.95). Covers all aspects of starting and running a small business; includes a section on coops.

Specialist topic publications

These go into considerable detail about one particular aspect.

Accounting and Financial Management for Charities, Hilary Blume and Michael Norton, Directory of Social Change, 1980 (£2.25).

Charitable status, A practical handbook, Andrew Phillips with Keith Smith, Inter-action, 1982 (£3.95). Step-by-step guide to registering a charity and a basic legal handbook for established charities.

The Charity Trading Handbook, Hilary Blume, Charity Trading Advisory Group, 1981 (£4.95) ref 39. Much of the detailed information is very relevant to small coops especially on developing a range of goods, mail order, thrift shops, and general marketing and selling practice.

Consumer Law for the Small Business, Patricia Clayton, Kogan Page, 1983 (£4.95). A comprehensive guide to consumer law written specifically for the small business.

Employers' Guide to National Insurance Contributions, DHSS (free).

Employment Law Affecting Workers' Cooperatives, Jim Brown, Beechwood, 1982 (£1.50) ref 15. Clear guide to main elements of employment law; deals in particular with contracts, grievance procedures and recruitment.

Export for the Small Business, Henry Deschampsneufs, Kogan Page, 1984 (£4.95). A guide to exporting which stresses the advantages of being small and shows that export is even possible without becoming involved directly with overseas customers.

Export Handbook, British Overseas Trade Board, HMSO, 1982, (£4.95). Detailed guide on all aspects of exporting.

Financial Management for the Small Business, Colin Barrow, Kogan Page, 1984 (£5.95). A practical guide for controlling finance and improving business performance.

Getting Sales Richard D Smith and Ginger Dick, Kogan Page, 1984 (£4.95). A book for all representatives and sales managers on getting more sales.

The Guardian Guide to Running a Small Business, 3rd edn, ed Clive Woodcock, Kogan Page, 1983 (£5.95). A series of clear, succinct and practical articles taken from the *Small Business Guardian.*

A Guide to the Benefits of Charitable Status, Michael Norton, Directory of Social Change, 1983 (£4.95).

If the Village Shop Closes, a handbook on community shops, Sue Gwilliam, Oxfordshire Rural Community Council, 1981 (£2.00).

Insurance Protection, ed Paula Pedlar, NCVO, 1983 (£2.00). Although written as a guide for voluntary organisations, this is equally useful for coop groups just starting up.

Law for the Small Business, 3rd edn, Patricia Clayton, Kogan Page, 1982 (£5.50). Every aspect of the law affecting the small business is treated clearly and succinctly.

Phoenix Cooperatives, Cooperative Development Agency, 1983 (£1.50) ref 1. A detailed guide on how to form a viable coop out of a redundancy situation.

Raising Finance, The Guardian Guide for the Small Business, Clive Woodcock, Kogan Page, 1982 (£4.95). A guide to the wide range of sources of finance available to small business.

Rights at Work. Jeremy McMullen, Pluto Press, 1979 (£2.95) A very detailed workers' guide to employment law.

Should I be Registered for VAT? HM Customs and Excise (free) ref 30.

Starting in Business. Inland Revenue (IR28) (free) ref 28.

Case studies

Finding out about what others have done is always a good way of learning. As there are still relatively few detailed case studies written about cooperatives we have listed as many as we are aware of.

Fakenham Enterprises, Martin Lockett, Cooperatives Research Unit, 1978 (£2.50) ref 17. Describes the setting up and eventual collapse of a workers' coop arising from a sit-in following the closure of a small shoe factory.

Fairblow Dynamics, Rob Paton, Cooperatives Research Unit, 1979 (£2.50) ref 17. Examines job satisfaction and people's attitudes in a medium-sized manufacturing company recently converted to common ownership.

Flagstone Enterprises Ltd, Local Government Unit and Local Enterprise Advisory Project, 1981 (£1.50). The setting up of a community business in a west of Scotland housing estate.

The Garment Cooperative, Chris Cornforth, Cooperatives Research Unit, 1981 (£2.00) ref 17, an experiment in industrial democracy and business creation. Story of a coop manufacturing woman's clothing set up after a factory closure using MSC Job Creation funds.

Little Pockets of Hope, Glen Buchanan, Local Government Unit and Local Enterprise Advisory Project, 1984 (£2.95). Story of Govan Workspace Ltd.

Little Women, Eirlys Tynan, Cooperatives Research Unit, 1980 (£1.50) ref 17. Describes the planning and setting up of a retail food shop by a group of married women in Sunderland.

Milkwood Cooperative Ltd, Rosemary Rhoades, Cooperatives Research Unit, 1980 (£2.00) ref 17. Brief history of a wood-working coop established under the MSC's Job Creation Programme and its failure to survive.

The Story of Neighbourhood Textiles, Tony Emerson, Cooperatives Research Unit, 1982 (£2.00) ref 17. Story of the unsuccessful attempt to promote 'from above' a small cooperatively owned textile business engaged in 'Cut Make and Trim'.

The Story of the Scottish Daily News, Ron McKay and Brian Barr, Canongate, 1976. The short life of the Glasgow newspaper coop which had to depend on a millionaire's cheque.

Sunderlandia, Eirlys Tynan, Cooperatives Research Unit, 1980 (£2.00) ref 17. The history of a (now closed) medium-sized firm in Sunderland.

Under New Management, Tony Eccles, Pan Books Ltd, 1981 (£2.95). Story of Britain's largest worker coop (Kirkby Manufacturing and Engineering) – its successes, failures and eventual collapse.

Unit 58, Eirlys Tynan, Cooperative Research Unit, 1980 (£1.00) ref 17. Brief description of a printing firm which traded for a while in Washington New Town.

What Business in the Port? Keith Hayton, Local Government Unit and Local Enterprise Advisory Project, 1984 (£2.95). Story of Port Glasgow Community Enterprises Ltd, a community-owned business involved in home craft production and furniture recycling.

Reference books

Croner's Reference Book for Employers, ed Shelagh Sweeney, Croner Publications Ltd (£30.40 plus £19.90 annual updating subscription). Comprehensive and regularly updated information service of legislation and regulations etc affecting employers.

Directory of Industrial and Service Cooperatives, Cooperative Development Agency, 1982 (£6.90) ref 1. Lists over 500 coops giving information on their activity, organisational structure, state of development, age, size and trading activity; revised annually.

Directory of Grant-making Trusts, ed Elizabeth Skinner, Charities Aid Foundation (£35.00).

Financial Resources for Economic Development (FRED), The Planning Exchange, Glasgow, (£20 Annual subscription, £60 to non-members) ref 34. Regularly updated comprehensive information service about financial schemes, legislation etc.

Handbook to the Industrial and Provident Societies Act and Supplements, W J Chappenden, Cooperative Union, 1966 (£5.00) ref 3.

Local Economic Development Information Service (LEDIS), The Planning Exchange, Glasgow (£7.50 Annual subscription, £25 to non-members) ref 34. Excellent regular single sheet information service on various aspects of local economic development including case histories of local projects; local authority initiatives; local advisory projects etc.

Index

171